HARLAXTON COLLEGE

R13665A0544

305.8/COM

D0860728

HARLAXTON COLLEGE LIBRARY
WITHDRAWN

ROOTS OF THE FUTURE

ETHNIC DIVERSITY IN THE MAKING OF BRITAIN

UNIVERSITY OF EVANSVILLE
HARLAXTON COLLEGE LIBRARY
HARLAXTON MANOR
GRANTHAM. LINCS.

UNITING BRITAIN

COMMISSION FOR
RACIAL EQUALITY

FOR A JUST SOCIETY

ACKNOWLEDGEMENTS

This book could not have been written without the generous help and advice we have received from numerous individuals and organisations. The Commission for Racial Equality would like to express its gratitude for their support and encouragement. In particular, it would like to thank Rozina Visram, who undertook initial research for the book; Jennie Karrach, who was responsible for the picture research; Annabel Ossel, who assisted with picture research; Michael Wyeld, who helped with the research and indexing; the Inter Faith Network for their advice and assistance; and Professor Colin Holmes of Sheffield University, who was especially generous with his time and expertise. Final responsibility for the publication, however, rests solely with the Commission for Racial Equality.

Writer and researcher: Mayerlene Frow
Designer: Louis Mackay
Editors: Matthew Brown, Judith Hanna
A great number of people at the Commission for Racial Equality have been involved in the *Roots of the Future* project, and thanks go to them all.

© Commission for Racial Equality
Elliot House
10-12 Allington Street
London SW1E 5EH

All rights reserved. No part of this publication may be reproduced, stored in a retrieval system or transmitted, in any form or by any means, electronic, mechanical, photographic, recorded or otherwise, without prior permission of the copyright owner.

First published 1996

ISBN 1 85442 179 4

Price £9.95

Printed by Belmont Press, Northampton

CONTENTS

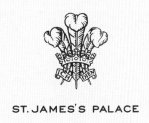

ST. JAMES'S PALACE

"Roots of the Future" is an imaginative initiative developed by the Commission for Racial Equality as part of its Uniting Britain for a Just Society Campaign. It aims to highlight the contributions and achievements made by immigrants and their descendants in almost every aspect of life in Britain. This contribution is incredibly wide and varied - from the economy, politics and the public service to the law, medicine, the arts and even our cooking. It is a contribution which today forms part of our national identity, and it adds immeasurably to the richness and creativity of modern Britain.

I am delighted to support this initiative, and I hope that it will not only enlighten and inform its readers, but also act as a spur to greater mutual understanding in the years to come.

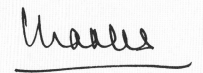

FOREWORD

Who am I?
Who are we?

To be British is to be part of a global network that encapsulates and transcends a variety of traditions and cultures. The people of Britain represent a commonwealth of different inheritances, backgrounds, influences, perspectives and experiences, and these are reflected in their own individual images of Britain.

Yet most of us know very little about each other or how people from such varied backgrounds have contributed, and are still contributing, to Britain's cultural, social and economic well-being.

A better understanding of the people of Britain will help us to appreciate and value the historic and contemporary contributions of all our citizens and residents, and recognise that they are an integral and invaluable part of the British nation.

Roots of the Future provides an illuminating insight into Britain's rich diversity. It is a small, initial, but significant step in understanding our modern, mixed society. It should help children and adults, students and tutors, citizens and politicians, employers and employees, leaders, followers, businesses, consumers, and those who are out of work to understand one another and see each other in more positive ways than we have up to now.

It has not been possible for this publication to cover all the positive contributions that are being made to Britain's cultural, economic and social development by its various people. Nevertheless, it provides people of all backgrounds and local communities with an opportunity to examine their own 'roots of the future' by looking closely at the many strands and contributions that make up their local cultures.

This is the beginning of an exciting project. It is about knowing each other better, valuing our differences, and understanding and respecting each other.

When questions are asked about Britain, its people, identity and, ultimately, belonging, we should have clear answers. Our goal should be a society in which we appreciate and value our differences, one where everyone can learn, work and live free from racial prejudice, discrimination, harassment and violence. That is the vision we must strive towards for Britain and all the people of Britain, as part of global cultural diversity.

I am what I am.
We are what we are.

Herman Ouseley
Chairman of the Commission for Racial Equality

INTRODUCTION

thnic diversity is nothing new in Britain. People with different histories, cultures, beliefs and languages have been coming here ever since the beginning of recorded time. Logically, therefore, everyone who lives in Britain today is either an immigrant or the descendant of an immigrant. Most of us can probably trace the immigrants in our own personal histories if we go back far enough.

People have come to Britain for many different reasons: some came peaceably, as settlers, others were hostile invaders. Thousands arrived as refugees from wars, famines, or civil or religious persecution in their own countries. Some were invited by the king or the government to settle here because they had particular skills that were in short supply in Britain. Some were brought against their will, as slaves or servants. Throughout the ages, Britain has been a magnet for those seeking a better life, in much the same way as Britons have emigrated, in large numbers, to other parts of the world. International movement has always been a normal part of life and, until 1914 when the First World War broke out, there were fewer restrictions. It was possible to travel to many countries without passports, visa requirements, or work permits. People could decide to make a new life somewhere else, provided they had money for the passage.

Over the centuries, there has also been considerable migration within Britain, for example between the separate countries of Scotland, England and Wales, which only became politically united as Great Britain in 1707; and between Ireland and the rest of Britain – even before Ireland became part of the United Kingdom in 1801, its proximity to England, Scotland and Wales meant that Irish people came over regularly in search of work. There was also migration between the countryside and the towns, so that by the end of the nineteenth century, two out of every five people in Britain lived in six or seven sprawling conurbations. For ease and consistency, we use the term Britain in this book, even though in some of the historical sections England, Scotland, Wales and Ireland would be more correct.

▲

A painted roll of a Westminster Tournament held in 1511 to celebrate the birth of a son to Catherine of Aragon. The black trumpeter, who is referred to in the salary accounts as John Blanke – it means John White, and was surely not his real name – was also employed in the court of Henry VII, and was paid 8d a day.

Ethnic diversity self-evidently involves the ethnic majorities – in Scotland, Wales, and England – as well as the ethnic minorities. In 1991, these majorities, themselves culturally and ethnically diverse, represented more than nine out of every ten people in Britain. Their complex histories and the contributions to British society and culture made by men and women such as Jane Austen, James Logie Baird, Alexander Graham Bell, William Blake, Robert Burns, Charles Dickens, Benjamin Britten, William Hogarth, D H Lawrence, Florence Nightingale, Thomas Paine, William Shakespeare, Dylan Thomas, Christopher Wren and thousands more, have been amply studied and appreciated. The purpose of this book, however, is to draw attention to the significant part played by people from Britain's ethnic minorities, and to emphasise the fact that many of the great names of British history and culture belong to immigrants or descendants of immigrants.

The term 'immigrant' is used in so many ways by politicians, journalists, economists and others that we must ask readers to be alert to various uses and misuses of the word. Officially, an immigrant is someone who arrives in a country, not as a visitor but as someone intending to remain for at least one year. Often, though, 'immigrant' is used to refer to anyone who is not white, even those who were born and brought up in Britain. The term 'ethnic minorities' is also sometimes used as though it meant 'immigrants', particularly immigrants who are not white. Usually, it excludes Americans and continental Europeans. An ethnic minority group is one whose members see themselves as sharing certain cultural characteristics, such as a common history, language, religion, or family or social values which distinguish them from the majority of the population. Greek-Cypriots, Germans, Irish, Polish and Italian communities in Britain are as much ethnic minorities as Jamaicans, Pakistanis, Bangladeshis, Somalis or Nigerians. If we mention the achievements of people from the second and third generations of British ethnic minorities in this book, this is not to suggest that they are 'new' to Britain, or even, in some cases, culturally distinct any longer, but to remind ourselves of the diverse cultural and ethnic origins that make up the British people.

Leaving aside such matters of definition, however, it may be asked, at what point does an immigrant and an immigrant's family become 'indigenous'? Settling into a new country and winning acceptance from the local population has always been a long and difficult process. There is no simple answer, and every individual will give a different reply, depending on his or her experience of settlement. A sense of belonging

This building at the corner of Brick Lane and Fournier Street in London's East End was built by Huguenot refugees in 1743 as a church. It later became a synagogue and is now used as a mosque by the Bengali community in Whitechapel. It stands today as a symbol of centuries of immigration to Britain.

ing grows out of the recognition, by individuals and society as a whole, that people from Britain's ethnic minorities are equally citizens and equally part of British culture, irrespective of their race or colour. It depends, too, on the ease which people from ethnic minorities feel in Britain, and the confidence they have that they can fulfil their potential just as easily as anyone else. Some immigrants, returning to their countries of origin after years of living in Britain, have discovered that the time they have spent away has gradually changed them, so much so that they do not feel completely at home there, and locals sometimes even dub them 'foreign-returned'.

In a sense, every newcomer to Britain encounters a different country. In the middle of the sixteenth century, the Protestant refugees who sought asylum in Britain found a predominantly agricultural society. They shared their skills and different perspectives with the British people and, in time, made important contributions towards the economic and technological development that helped to bring about the industrial revolution. Over three hundred years later, Jewish refugees fleeing to Britain from economic hardship and pogroms in feudal Tsarist Russia found a radically transformed industrial society. Britain had become the centre of an empire covering vast areas of the globe. And British culture was a product of the diverse cultural ingredients that had been added over the years to the national pot by immigrants and visitors, and by trade, travel and conquest.

Sometimes, the give and take between local British people and ethnic minorities has led, in time, to the gradual assimilation of cultural differences. Both minorities and majorities learn from each other, and the culture they share is subtly changed by the new assumptions and values they have imperceptibly negotiated. Even where people from ethnic minorities have preserved some of their distinctive cultural and religious traditions and values, the same process of adapting to life in Britain goes on, leaving neither the minority nor the majority populations untouched.

2

'Foreigners' have always been a tiny proportion of the British population. Even today, only about 7% of the population were not born in Britain, and 61% of these people are white. The remaining 'non-white' population are British-born. Partly because newcomers have usually settled in certain cities and regions, some local people have always imagined that they were 'taking over the country'. Occasionally, their hostility has erupted in riots and conflict. This has been one factor in persuading governments to introduce immigration controls. Even a cursory examination would show that immigrants are among the more productive citizens. Some have brought skills and qualifications that are in scarce supply; others have set up businesses and created work, not only for themselves but also for local people; and many have been willing to do jobs that employers have found difficulty in filling locally. What is remarkable, and often not understood, is how much immigrants have contributed, and continue to contribute, to Britain. It is so easy to see if only we are prepared to look.

The aim of this book is to show that Britain has benefited enormously from immigration and ethnic diversity throughout history. Immigrants, with the fresh perspective they bring as outsiders, are often a catalyst for change. Far from impoverishing the country, as some still claim, immigrants have brought new blood, in many senses.

The book is divided into two parts. The first gives a very brief account of the role played by a few of the migrant communities who came to Britain and settled here before the end of the Second World War. We outline the contributions they have made to Britain's economic, social, political and cultural development, and the difficulties and obstacles they have faced, and overcome, in the process. The second part focuses on the fifty years since the end of the Second World War. It is a selection of snapshots of key areas of society where immigration and ethnic diversity have enriched life in Britain. The bibliography lists all the books and articles that we have used to draw together the information on which this book is based.

▲
Young people in Britain today are growing up in an ethnically and racially diverse society. They know no other.

No single book can hope to cover all the contributions made by all immigrants and their descendants to Britain – that would require volumes, even libraries. Our one regret is that we can give only a flavour of the extraordinary range of activities and achievements involved. For every individual we refer to as an example, there are hundreds of thousands for whom there is no space. Nor is this book intended to be a comprehensive survey of the *presence* of the different ethnic minority communities who have lived in Britain at various times. There are already some excellent histories of many ethnic minority communities, and local historians have uncovered a wealth of information about immigrants and settlers in particular localities. Our much more modest aim is to give a glimpse, necessarily fleeting and impressionistic, of the history and value of ethnic diversity in Britain. We shall have achieved a great deal more if our project serves as a spur to others to examine more thoroughly the dynamic role ethnic minorities have played throughout history in the making of Britain, and the way they have enriched its economic, social and cultural life.

1

IMMIGRANTS PAST AND PRESENT

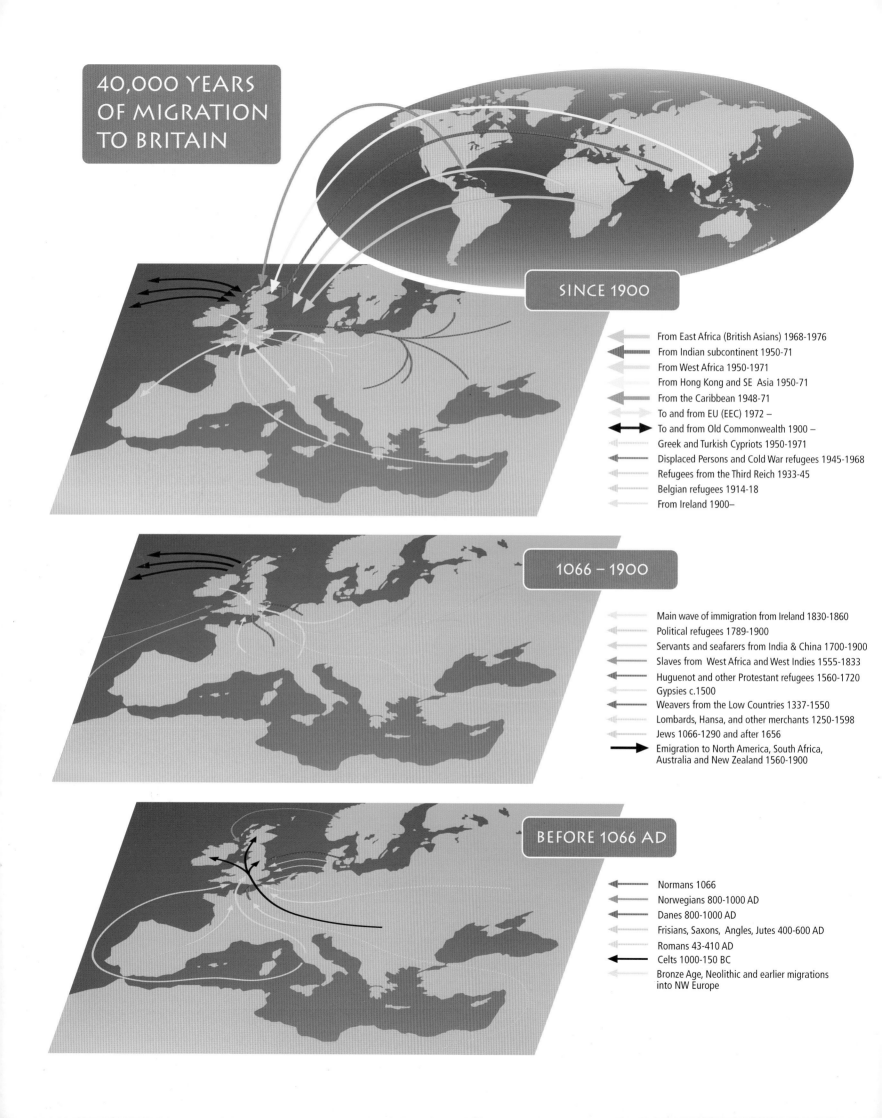

40,000 YEARS OF MIGRATION TO BRITAIN

SINCE 1900

From East Africa (British Asians) 1968-1976
From Indian subcontinent 1950-71
From West Africa 1950-1971
From Hong Kong and SE Asia 1950-71
From the Caribbean 1948-71
To and from EU (EEC) 1972 –
To and from Old Commonwealth 1900 –
Greek and Turkish Cypriots 1950-1971
Displaced Persons and Cold War refugees 1945-1968
Refugees from the Third Reich 1933-45
Belgian refugees 1914-18
From Ireland 1900–

1066 – 1900

Main wave of immigration from Ireland 1830-1860
Political refugees 1789-1900
Servants and seafarers from India & China 1700-1900
Slaves from West Africa and West Indies 1555-1833
Huguenot and other Protestant refugees 1560-1720
Gypsies c.1500
Weavers from the Low Countries 1337-1550
Lombards, Hansa, and other merchants 1250-1598
Jews 1066-1290 and after 1656
Emigration to North America, South Africa, Australia and New Zealand 1560-1900

BEFORE 1066 AD

Normans 1066
Norwegians 800-1000 AD
Danes 800-1000 AD
Frisians, Saxons, Angles, Jutes 400-600 AD
Romans 43-410 AD
Celts 1000-150 BC
Bronze Age, Neolithic and earlier migrations into NW Europe

THE EARLIEST IMMIGRANTS

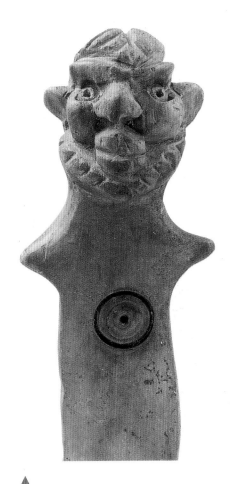

This carved wooden spoon handle, dating from the first century AD and found buried 15 feet below Southwark Bridge in London, is one of a number of archaeological finds from the Roman period in Britain indicating the presence of people of African origin. Among the troops defending Hadrian's Wall in the third century was a 500-strong 'division of Moors'.

L ittle is known about the first people who inhabited the land we now call Britain, except that they came from somewhere else. They were immigrants. Early stone, bronze and ceramic finds suggest that the culture of the migrants, who came by way of north-west Europe, shared common features with peoples from as far away as the Mediterranean and the Near East.

During the first millennium BC, Celts, originally descended from dwellers on the Russian steppes, first arrived in the British Isles from central Europe and, over the centuries, merged with the original population. Their language shared a common root with other 'Indo-European' languages – a family that includes French, German, Russian, Greek, Persian and Sanskrit, and from which Hindi, Punjabi, Bengali and Gujarati are derived. Land and sea trade routes linking Britain with the Mediterranean were already well established during this period.

In the first century AD, Celtic Britain south of Hadrian's Wall became part of the vast Roman Empire which extended deep into the Middle East and north Africa. The Romans ruled Britain for 400 years, and built its first substantial cities, roads and ports. In the early fifth century, after the Romans abandoned Britain, there was a succession of large-scale invasions by people from what is now northern Germany, southern Denmark, and the northern part of the Netherlands – Angles, Saxons, Jutes and Frisians. A synthesis of Germanic culture and language known as Anglo-Saxon soon became dominant in the south and the east of what may, for the first time, be called England: Angle-land, or the land of the Angles.

Meanwhile, the surviving Celtic culture became confined to Scotland, Wales and the southwest of England. Fresh invasions and migrations from Scandinavia, from the ninth century, left strong traces of Norse culture in the population, language and culture, especially in the north of England and Scotland, and for two hundred years there were skirmishes and compromises between the descendants of Scandinavians in the north and the Anglo-Saxons in the south. In 1016, Cnut, a Dane, became King of England. The Norman invasion of 1066 marked the defeat of the Saxons, and brought French culture and language to England. The language we speak today has grown from a mixture of Saxon, Norse and Norman-French tongues.

All the subsequent immigration to Britain has been relatively peaceful, and has involved smaller proportions of people compared to the great movements of the past. Indeed, the last ten centuries have seen more emigration by Britons than immigration.

The Norman landings in 1066 were depicted a few years after the event on the Bayeux tapestry. The Viking fleets which had already been coming to Britain for over two hundred years would have had much the same appearance.

THE FIRST JEWISH COMMUNITY

The first Jewish settlements in Britain date back to the Norman Conquest in 1066, when William the Conqueror encouraged Jews to come to Britain from France with the offer of royal protection. By the end of the thirteenth century, there were Jewish populations in 27 centres including London, Norwich, Canterbury, Oxford, Cambridge, Exeter, Lincoln, and York. The Jews formed tightly-knit communities, and distinctive ones. They were forbidden by the Church to own land, to employ Christians, or to carry arms. Most occupations were therefore closed to them because of their religion. Since Christians were forbidden to lend money for interest, moneylending became one of the few means of income open to Jews. It made them indispensable to the king, whose coffers needed constant replenishing. While the Jewish community did not live as a completely separate group, they lived near to each other, and to the royal castles upon whose protection they depended.

In a society where the power of the Church was felt in every corner of life, and sermons regularly reinforced the message that usury was a sin, Jews were a source of finance at every level, from the purchase of a cow to the kings' crusades. They also paid for the construction of some of Britain's magnificent cathedrals, abbeys and castles. Most Jews were small moneylenders, pawnbrokers rather than financiers, and only a few, like Aaron of Lincoln, made a considerable amount of money. However, the taxes and fines imposed on the Jewish community through a special department called the Exchequer of the Jews, became so extortionate that even the rich were reduced to ruin. In the ten years between 1263 and 1273, Edward I extracted £420,000 from the Jewish community.

Popular resentment against Jews was widespread, partly because people envied the royal protection they received, partly because they were not Christians, and partly because of the interest they charged on their loans. Stereotyping Jews as grasping

▶

Jewish merchants in medieval England. In 1275, Edward I issued a decree that every Jew had to wear a piece of yellow taffeta six fingers long and three broad as a badge of identification. A similar requirement was revived over six and a half centuries later in Nazi Germany, where Jews were ordered to identify themselves by wearing a Star of David.

moneylenders made them easy targets for all kinds of popular grievances and religious superstitions. In London in 1189 there was a riot when Jews tried to enter the Cathedral to give Richard I a gift at his coronation. Thirty Jews were killed, and Jewish houses burned down. Riots broke out in Bury St Edmunds and York, where the barons decided to wipe out their debts by killing their creditors. Clifford's Tower in York, where some 150 Jews had taken refuge from a besieging mob, was set on fire – the ruins still stand today. The kings spent money faster than Jews could raise it and, in

Aaron of Lincoln helped finance the
building of Lincoln Cathedral, as well as
Peterborough Cathedral, St Alban's Abbey
and nine Cistercian monasteries.

1290, when Jews were no longer useful as a source of revenue, their property was confiscated and they were expelled. At its peak, the Jewish population in the early thirteenth century has been put at about 5,000, or 0.025% of the estimated population of England. As the founders of banking, financial and insurance services, the Jews provided a system of credit in a society where there were no banks as we know them today.

It was another 366 years before Judaism could be legally practised in Britain. Oliver Cromwell was persuaded by a delegation of Sephardi Jews from Spain and Portugal in 1656 that Britain could benefit from their commercial and financial skills, and their capital, as it had done before. The 'readmission' brought families such as the Henriques, the Francias and the Da Costas, who were among the leading merchants of their day.

Georg Gisze was a merchant from the Hanseatic city of Danzig (now Gdansk in Poland). Hans Holbein's picture shows him at his desk in the London Steelyard. The inscription on the wall gives Gisze's age as 34, and his motto in Latin, 'No joy without sorrow'. Holbein, born in Augsburg, was appointed court painter at Henry VIII's court in 1526. He was the first in a line of continental painters to work for English royal patrons. His successors in the seventeenth century included Sir Anthony Van Dyck, Daniel Mytens and Sir Peter Lely.

MERCHANTS AND CRAFTWORKERS

Jews were not the only foreigners in Britain in the early medieval period. European merchants, familiar visitors to London before the Norman conquest, were arriving in increasing numbers, especially from the Low Countries, Germany and Lombardy in Italy – Lombard Street in London still recalls their presence. They gradually replaced Jews as the country's financiers.

Besides capital, however, the most crucial ingredient needed to make Britain more productive and competitive at that time was technical knowledge: in metals, mining, agriculture, engineering, crafts of every description and, most of all, textiles. In the fourteenth century, wool was one of Britain's major exports. However, the variety of imports – cloth among them – was a measure of how far Britain lagged behind the countries of the continent in economic development. In 1337, Edward III issued a proclamation promising 'all cloth workers of strange lands, of whatsoever country they be' the King's protection and safe conduct, and offering them tax exemptions if they came.

Some of the manufacturing skills and techniques were provided by Flemish and French weavers, German mining engineers, Italian glass manufacturers, Dutch canal builders, brewers, printers, paper manufacturers and brickmakers. In addition, the immigrants brought with them new types of industrial organisation: craft guilds, which were the precursors of trade unions, and employers' associations.

In 1440, when Richard II decided to tax all aliens (except wealthy merchants and servants), there were about 16,000 foreigners in England, approximately 1% of the population. There was even then a common misapprehension that the country was being flooded by 'strangers', and that they were getting special treatment over the king's own subjects – a familiar complaint throughout history.

▲

Papermaking was one of the industries that Dutch craftworkers helped to develop in England.

So many Easterlings,
Lombards and Flemings
To bear away our winnings
Saw I never

(John Skelton, 1512)

◄

A weaver at her loom. In the fifteenth century, 90% of England's exports were wool and woollen cloth. In exchange, the country imported silks, velvets and spices from Genoa, leather and iron from Spain, linen from Flanders and wine from Gascony. England also imported skilled weavers from the Low Countries – now Belgium, the Netherlands, and parts of northern France and Germany.

A late medieval image
symbolising crafts and industry gives a
vivid sense of the world in which
immigrant craftworkers lived
and worked.

Local hostility, however, was directed less at the craftsmen, who had much to teach, than at the foreign favourites at court, the very wealthy Lombard merchants, and the merchants of the Hanseatic League – a loose trading association of German and Baltic towns. A few concessions were made to allay popular feeling; the number of foreign apprentices was restricted in 1484, and the Hansa merchants were gradually squeezed out between 1556 and 1598 when the Steelyard, the warehouse near London Bridge from which they operated, was closed down. In 1601, Elizabeth I also ordered the Lord Mayor of London to expel the tiny black population of runaway slaves that had sprung up out of the lucrative slave trade in Africa which was just beginning at the time. The economy, however, still depended heavily on imports, and the skills of foreigners. Immigration was useful and was not discouraged.

PROTESTANT REFUGEES

The sixteenth century was a time of religious wars in Europe, following the rejection of the authority of the Roman Catholic church sparked by Martin Luther, John Calvin, and other 'Protestants'. Between 1550 and 1660 thousands of highly skilled Protestant refugees found safety in Britain from savage religious persecution in the Low Countries and France. Their loss was Britain's gain, although some thought otherwise – 'Tottenham is turned Flemish' was all the cry, and Bermondsey was dubbed 'Petty Burgundy'.

These immigrants played a revolutionary role in manufacturing. Besides importing new weaving techniques – the new soft draperies became much more popular than the heavy British woollen cloth – they also introduced improved techniques in printing; glass engraving; brick manufacture; wire, paper, salt and soap making; copper, silver and lead mining; leather work; pottery; horticulture; and canal engineering. Houses were increasingly made of brick and, thanks to waterwheels set up on one of the arches of London Bridge in 1582 by Pieter Morice, a German immigrant, water from the Thames was pumped to Londoners' homes through lead pipes instead of being carted by water carriers. Dutch beer was so popular that the English word 'brewhouse' was replaced by the Dutch 'brewery'.

Despite popular resentment, there was, even at this time, some appreciation of what the immigrants were contributing. An observer in Sandwich, which was 'almost transformed into a Flemish town with windmills', wrote in the 1590s of 'the great advantage' they had brought 'by the increase of inhabitants, the employment of the poor and the money which circulated'.

Between 1680 and 1720, many highly skilled Calvinist refugees fled from persecution in France. In 1700, there were about 50,000 newcomers, about 1% of England's estimated population of five or six million. The Huguenots, as they were known, settled mainly in London and the south-east, and had an important centre in Spitalfields. They were initially made welcome – in 1686, £50,000 was raised through an appeal to help them – but resentment grew at the advantage they gained from their 'machines for working of tape, lace, ribbon and such, wherein one man doth more among them than seven Englishe men can doe', which 'beggareth all our English artificers of that trade and enricheth them'.

The Huguenots brought with them the arts of making crystal, fine paper (which made possible the printing of paper money), dyes, watches and clocks, spectacles and scientific instruments, boots, hats and wigs, and silk. At one time, in the late eighteenth century, there were 12,000 silk looms in Spitalfields alone, producing silk, velvet and brocades which had previously been imported. Many Huguenots were scientists and became Fellows of the Royal Society. In 1682, Denis

When the Dutch engineer, Sir Cornelius Vermuyden, and his team were employed by the Earl of Bedford to drain the Fens, there were loud protests. But by 1637, large areas of land that had previously been swamp had become the productive farmland it is today.

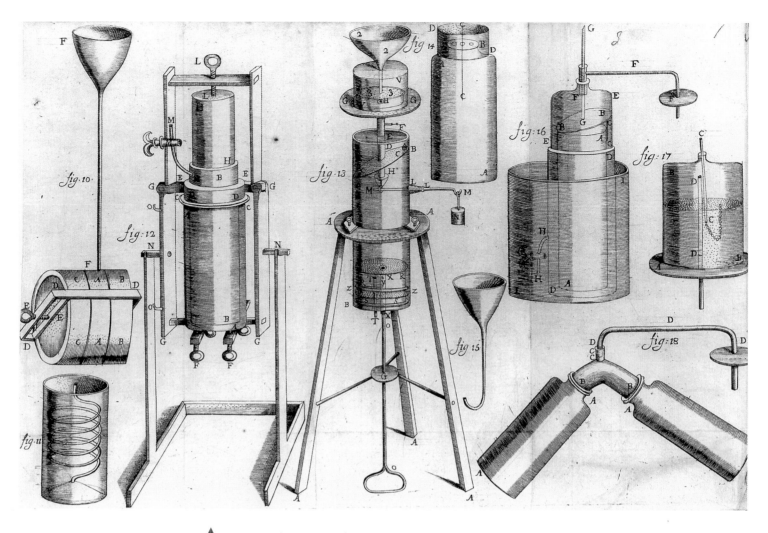

Denis Papin's 'digester of bones' – the first pressure cooker.

An engraved gold watch made by the Huguenot watchmaker, James Tregent, in 1767. The Courtauld family, whose son Samuel set up the famous textile works, were also well-known gold and silver smiths.

Papin gave a demonstration of the pressure cooker he had invented, and John Dollond, whose name still survives in the opticians, Dollond and Aitchison, improved the design of the telescope and microscope. There were also distinguished writers, scholars and artists among them, who broadened the nation's intellectual life.

Like the Jews and Lombards, the Huguenots played a vital role in the development of banking. Jonathan's Coffee House in Change Alley became the centre of their activities. Sir John Houblon, the son of a Huguenot refugee, was elected the first governor of the Bank of England in 1694.

The Huguenots set up their own schools, charities and the first friendly societies in the country. They also had their own churches, 23 in London alone in 1700. They were jealous of their independence, but in time, both newcomers and natives changed, learning from each other and gradually becoming part of a new and richer culture. By this time, the British people were a mixture of far more than Celt, Anglo-Saxon, Dane, and Norman ancestry. Names still allow us to trace the centuries of foreign immigrants who settled in Britain. Surnames such as Fleming, Olivier, Dekker, and Burke belonged to Dutch people, Huguenots and Normans, and the name of a pub in Colchester, 'Goat and Boots', is a corruption of the Dutch words, 'der Goden Boode' ('messenger of the gods'), seen on Dutch inn signs. For a relatively small population, the Huguenots had an immense impact on the society they had joined.

HIGH LIFE AND STREET LIFE

The eighteenth century did not see any substantial immigration to Britain. Most newcomers came as individuals or small groups. Among the upper classes, it was an age of abundant wealth, show and extravagance. Trade was flourishing and the estates of country gentlemen were lavishly decorated by Italian artists. London, with the court at its centre, became a lure for anyone with the talent to satisfy the insatiable craving for novelty. The success of the Tories at the general election of 1710 committed the country to the Protestant succession of the House of Hanover on the death of Queen Anne. It was to this court that one of Britain's greatest composers, the German immigrant, George Frederick Handel, came in 1712. Heidegger, his Swiss partner, became one of the foremost theatre producers of the age, while Philippe de Loutherbourg revolutionised stage scenery. Clementi, the pianoforte manufacturer, is credited with composing the first piano pieces, and Johann Christian, son of the famous organist Johann Sebastian Bach, who was drawn to London by Handel's presence, became known as the 'English Bach'. Jonathan Swift, Edmund Burke and Richard Brinsley Sheridan, immigrants from Ireland, were among the intellectual and literary giants of the age.

Irish people continued to arrive as seasonal agricultural workers and casual labourers, as they had done for centuries. There were probably no more than 14,000 in England altogether, settled mainly in certain parts of London, but they suffered continual harassment and persecution. There were anti-Irish riots in London in 1736, and anti-Catholic sentiment exploded again in 1780 in the Gordon Riots. The trade in

George Frederick Handel, the German composer, counted among his friends and admirers some of the leading writers and artists of the day – Henry Fielding, Alexander Pope and William Hogarth. Handel began by writing operas, but responded to the change in musical fashion by composing oratorios and choral works such as the *Messiah,* as well as orchestral compositions such as the *Music for the Royal Fireworks.* A rehearsal by 100 musicians on 21 April 1749 was heard by an audience of 12,000. This terracotta bust is by the Huguenot sculptor, François Roubilliac.

A cup of tea in Covent Garden market in eighteenth century London.

Antonio Canaletto (1687-1768) lived in London for many years in the eighteenth century, and his paintings, like this one of Whitehall, give us a vivid impression of the city at the time.

African slaves, which had started in the reign of Elizabeth I, was fully established by the eighteenth century, and there was a small population of about 15,000 black people in London by 1700. It nevertheless prompted the *Daily Journal* to warn its readers on 5 April 1723:

> Tis said there is a great number of Blacks come daily into this City, so that 'tis thought in a short time, if they be not suppress'd, the City will swarm with them.

Gypsies probably arrived in England during the early decades of the sixteenth century. They made a living as tinkers, pedlars, horse dealers and street entertainers, but faced constant persecution because of their distinctive nomadic culture and their perceived racial difference. In the 1650s, Gypsies were performing in plays near Edinburgh and were lodged in the castle. The 1562 Egyptian Act, by which Elizabeth I had sought to expel them, was repealed in 1783, and it was no longer legal to persecute Gypsies just because they were Gypsies. However, the broad scope of the 1824 Vagrancy Act, and various Hawkers and Pedlars Acts, allowed all itinerants to be cruelly hounded.

Early in the eighteenth century, Yiddish-speaking Ashkenazi Jews began to arrive from eastern Europe. They were distinct in many ways from the Sephardi Jews already settled in Britain. Most made their living as pedlars, secondhand clothes dealers, tailors, shoemakers and artisans, because they were still barred from other trades. By 1750, they outnumbered the Sephardi Jews by four to one. A Bill giving Jewish children rights of naturalisation in 1753 aggravated the strong anti-alien sentiment in the country, and the cry was 'No Jews, No Wooden Shoes'. Even Huguenots, long settled in Britain, did not escape the hostility towards foreigners. There were some, however, who saw the stupidity of prejudice. In the 1660s, Samuel Pepys, the diarist, deplored 'the absurd nature of Englishmen who could not forebear laughing and jeering at anything that looks strange.' A hundred years later, in 1762, Oliver Goldsmith, the Anglo-Irish poet, found the English 'full of superior pride, impatience and a peculiar hardness of soul'. They were 'brutish towards one another and inevitably, therefore, to strangers. Foreigners find themselves ridiculed and insulted in every street.'

The casual work performed by Jews, Irish, Africans and Gypsies in the informal economy was not of marginal significance. In a society where the overwhelming majority of the population were illiterate, the only way people could get news was through broadsheet vendors or ballad singers, and the street minstrels provided an invaluable news service, as well as a great deal of pleasure to those who could not afford a ticket at the Opera House. As rag dealers, tinkers and pedlars, they recycled goods and made them more widely available by selling them cheaply at fairs and markets all over the country.

SLAVES AND SUBJECTS

People in Britain during the seventeenth and eighteenth centuries can hardly have been unaware of the trade in African slaves. British traders and manufacturers made fortunes through what has become known as the triangular trade. Ships left Bristol and Liverpool laden with textiles from Lancashire, cutlery and muskets from Birmingham, and other goods, including beer brewed by Samuel Whitbread and Sir Benjamin Truman. On the West African coast, these were traded for slaves, who were then transported across the Atlantic to Barbados, Jamaica and Surinam and sold to plantation owners. The ships were then loaded with sugar, cotton, spices, rum and tobacco for sale in Britain.

In his book, *Staying Power,* Peter Fryer quotes an estimate of the net overall profits to British slave merchants on 2,500,000 Africans bought and sold between 1630 and 1807 as being about £12 million (half of this was made between 1750 and 1790). To a large extent, capital accumulated from the slave trade allowed Britain to become the first country to experience an industrial revolution, and secured the fortunes of traders, brokers and bankers. Many of them were Huguenots, who had a large stake in the overseas expansion which was under way. Some were shareholders of the East India Company. Liverpool shipowners accounted for 60% of the English slave trade, and 40% of Europe's.

Slaves were also bought and sold openly in Britain, especially in Bristol and Liverpool, where street names such as Negro Row and Black Boy Lane still carry echoes of the cruel trade. There were 61 taverns in London called Black Boy and 51 called Blackamoore's Head. However, most of the black population in Britain came as slaves belonging to ship captains, plantation owners and others. Some arrived as stowaways, escaping from the horrors of plantation life. After the American War of Independence a small number of black people, who had been promised freedom if they fought for Britain, came here. By 1787, the black population in London had risen to 20,000.

It was very fashionable towards the end of the eighteenth century to have black

A carving of an African head from Liverpool Town Hall. Liverpool accounted for about 60% of the English slave trade, which explains the significance of the following election squib in 1790:

If our slave trade had gone,
*   there's an end to our lives*
Beggars all we must be,
*   our children and wives*
No ships from our ports
*   their proud sails e'er will spread*
And our streets grown with grass,
*   where the cows might be fed.*

RUN away from his Master on the 2d Instant, David Marat, a Black about seventeen Years of Age, with short wooly Hair ; He had on a whitish Cloath Livery, Lin'd with Blew, and Princes-mettal Buttons, with a Turbant on his Head : He sounds a Trumpet, whoever secures him and brings him to Edward Talbot Esq ; by Kingstreet near Soho, shall have five Guines Reward.

18th century advertisement for a runaway servant.

Henrietta of Lorraine, by Sir Anthony Van Dyck. The imperious Henrietta appears to have stopped her servant on his way somewhere. He looks up startled, but deeply deferential. Black servants appear in countless seventeenth and eighteenth century paintings, nearly always as a foil to the main figures. In some they are grouped with the family's pets or horses, whose status in the household they shared.

Above left: A concert in 1794. Above right: A detail from Hogarth's *Captain Graham in his cabin*. Music was one field in which black people could get employment during the eighteenth and nineteenth centuries. Many served as drummers in the army and on ships. A black drummer accompanied the Household Cavalry into the Battle of Blenheim in 1704.

and Indian servants, as paintings of the time show. Some exceptional individuals became well known – men such as Larbe, who was fluent in several languages, and Soubise, who became the Duchess of Queensbury's fencing master. Others found work as drummers in military regiments, risking life and limb as they led soldiers into the fray. During the last decade of the eighteenth century, all the drummers of the Royal Fusiliers were African. Yet like the Jews, Gypsies, and Irish before them, the vast majority of black people, even free men, were barred from becoming apprentices to a trade, and were obliged to make their living as pedlars, pugilists or street entertainers. They joined the numerous other nationalities on the streets – Italians in particular – who were trying to make an 'honest living by scraping the cat gut'. Joseph Johnson attracted audiences as much by the model of a ship which he sported on his hat as by his repertoire of popular English songs. A report in an 1823 broadsheet of the funeral procession of one-legged Billy Waters, who busked outside the Adelphi Theatre in the Strand in London, leaves little doubt as to the size of his fan club.

Hints of the talents that were suppressed by the barbarism of slavery, and the racist doctrines invented to protect it, survive in the records of the fortunate few black people who were able to fulfil some of their potential, and whose names are still celebrated. Among them was Ignatius Sancho, who ran a fashionable grocery shop in Westminster, and counted among his friends writers such as Laurence Sterne, author of *Tristram Shandy*; Samuel Johnson, author of a famous dictionary; and David Garrick, the actor. Another, Olaudah Equiano, published his 'best-selling' autobiography, and campaigned tirelessly against the slave trade.

Olaudah Equiano's autobiography went into nine editions in his lifetime and was translated into Dutch and German. In the USA, his book was a powerful influence on the writings of Frederick Douglass, the runaway slave who took England by storm in 1845, as well as on the work of black US writers such as Booker T Washington, Richard Wright, James Baldwin and Ralph Ellison.

Funeral Procession of Poor "BLACK BILLY."

A broadsheet of 1823 conveys the popularity of the black street musician, Billy Waters.

Ottobah Cugoano, a servant to the court painter, Cosway, also published an attack on the slave trade in 1787. Tom Molineaux and James Wharton were among the champion boxers of their times; while in the nineteenth century, William Cuffay became a leading member of the Chartist movement, which campaigned to secure universal suffrage (for men), equal representation in Parliament and abolition of the need to own property in order to be eligible for a seat in Parliament. James Africanus Beale Horton, from Sierra Leone, graduated in medicine from London and Edinburgh universities, was appointed an army medical officer, and rose to the rank of major. Horton's most important book was *A Vindication of the African Race*. Mary Seacole's services as a nurse during the Crimean War were recognised in her own time, and were widely publicised by *Punch* magazine and *The Times's* war correspondent, W H Russell. She was the first woman to enter Sebastopol when it fell, 'laden with wine, bandages and food for the wounded'.

Signs of the success of Britain's other major overseas trading venture, in India, were already beginning to appear with returning English and Scottish 'nabobs' flaunting their wealth and their Indian servants. Between 1757 and 1771 the East India Company and its servants received about £30 million from Indian princes and subjects through 'wanton oppression' and 'flagitious cruelties'. The company sent Warren Hastings out to set things right. At a more humble level, Chinese, Indian, Somali, and Yemeni 'lascars' – seamen recruited by British merchant ships for the homeward journey to Britain – began to appear in British ports in the eighteenth century. In 1858, the year when the East India Company was abolished and India was brought under the direct rule of the British Crown, the first branches of Indian firms were set up in London – Cama and Co, a Parsi cotton firm, and Sassoons, an Iraqi Jewish financial firm, both from Bombay, came first. Another Parsi firm, Tata Iron and Steel Co, followed soon afterwards.

Long before the end of the nineteenth century, the success of the British Empire depended crucially on the labour of some two million Indian and Chinese 'indentured' workers on contracts who had replaced the slaves emancipated in 1833 in the colonies and dominions. The contract labourers worked on sugar plantations in Fiji and the West Indies, in the mines of South Africa, on the rubber plantations of Malaya, on the railroads in East Africa, and in the police and armed services in Kenya, Burma and elsewhere.

▶ Sake Deen Mahomed and his 'Shampooing Baths' in Brighton. Shampooing was a massage technique used to cure asthma and rheumatism. He was the first Indian author to publish a book in English – *Travels of Deen Mahomet* – in Cork, where he first lived after arriving from India in 1784 in the service of one Captain Baker. But he made his reputation by shampooing famous people such as Lord Castlereagh, Robert Peel, and King George IV. Mahomed died in 1851.

▲ Mary Seacole, sculpted by a nephew of Queen Victoria, showing the medals she received for her work in the Crimea. A four-day musical festival was organised in her honour at the Royal Surrey Gardens in Kennington, with 1000 performers and nine military bands.

▲ Indian ayahs, or nannies, in Glasgow at the beginning of this century.

Chinese sailors unloading tea. ▶

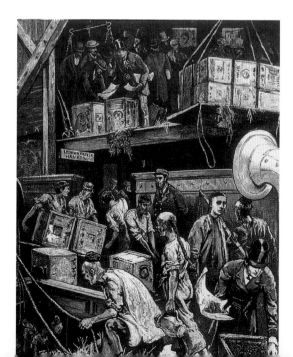

INDUSTRIALISTS, BANKERS AND POLITICAL EMIGRÉS

An early paint bottle from the Berger paint company, set up in the eighteenth century by Louis Steigenberger.

In the middle of the eighteenth century, there were about 4,000 Germans settled in Britain, many of them professionals with sophisticated financial and industrial skills, who played a vital role in Britain's industrial and economic development. Francis Baring, son of a cloth manufacturer from Bremen, set up Baring Brothers in 1770, the most powerful banking house in Europe at the time. He was also director and chairman of the East India Company. Another immigrant from Bremen, Andreas Grote, also set up a bank in 1776. Louis Steigenberger from Frankfurt specialised in the production of chemical dyes. He changed his name to Berger, which survives today on tins of Berger Paints.

By 1914, the German population in Britain had risen to about 40,000, partly encouraged by Queen Victoria's marriage to a Hanoverian, Prince Albert. Among the numerous industrialists, two were especially prominent. In 1873, Ludwig Mond, a German Jew, and T J Brunner, the son of a Swiss pastor in Liverpool, teamed up to start what grew into Britain's largest chemical enterprise, Imperial Chemical Industries (ICI). Karl Siemens, who came to London from Hanover in 1852, started manufacturing telegraphic equipment cables and insulators eight years later, and set up a steelworks in Birmingham in 1867.

The first – and certainly not the last – American to come to Britain in 1616 was Pocahontas. US immigrants set up banks (J P Morgan), hotels (Waldorf Astor), department stores (Gordon Selfridge), charitable housing estates for the poor (George Peabody), and helped finance the Northern, Bakerloo and Piccadilly Underground lines in London (Charles Tyson Yerkes). Henry Wellcome and Silas Burroughs, also from the USA, established a pharmaceutical company, which was taken over in January 1996 by Glaxo Pharmaceuticals, itself originally a firm set up by the son of a Jewish immigrant jobbing tailor at the end of the nineteenth century.

Jewish immigrants played a vital role in merchant banking. Prominent among them was the House of Rothschild, which helped to finance the British effort in the Napoleonic Wars, and provided funds at short notice for the British Government's purchase of Suez Canal shares in 1875. Nathan de Rothschild, the first member of the family to arrive in Manchester from Frankfurt in 1799 as a textile exporter, became a leading spokesman in Britain on financial matters. It is claimed that he was the first man in the country to know of the victory at Waterloo. However, it still took years of campaigning before his son, Lionel, could take his seat in Parliament. The House of Rothschild serves as a gold broker to the Bank of England even today. Among other notable Jewish merchant banking families were the Samuel Montagues,

Lionel de Rothschild at the Zoo he founded in Tring.

Victor Hugo spent 18 years as an exile in Guernsey. *Les Misérables* and *Toilers of the Sea*, which is set in Guernsey, were published before he returned to France in 1870.

▼

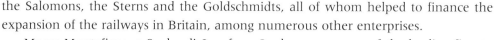

the Salomons, the Sterns and the Goldschmidts, all of whom helped to finance the expansion of the railways in Britain, among numerous other enterprises.

Moses Montefiore, a Sephardi Jew from Leghorn, was one of the leading figures in the diamond trade, an area of strong Jewish interest since the 1660s when the East India Company opened access to the Indian markets. He was also committed to the cause of full civil liberty for Jewish people, became Sheriff of London in 1837 and was knighted by Queen Victoria in the same year. Other leading trading families of the time were the Francos (also in the diamond trade), the Mocadas and Goldschmids (in silver bullion), and the Brandons (in tobacco). As the historian, Eric Hobsbawm, remarks, even at the turn of the century when Britain's place as the world's leading industrial nation was being overtaken by Germany and the USA:

> The rare dynamic entrepreneurs of Edwardian Britain were, more often than not, foreigners or minority groups; the increasingly important German-Jewish financiers (who provided the excuse for much of the pervasive anti-semitism of the period), the Americans, so important in the electrical industry, and the Germans in chemicals.

The chaotic succession of revolutions and restorations in Europe following the French revolution in 1789 brought some 80,000 temporary refugees, including some of the greatest intellectuals, industrialists, artists and scholars of their age, or any other. Among the exiles who found sanctuary in Britain in the nineteenth century were: Antonio Panizzi, the Italian who worked as a senior librarian at the British Museum, and designed its magnificent reading room – its copper dome is one of the largest in the world; Karl Marx, the German political economist and philosopher, who wrote about contemporary politics and society in Britain and set up the first International Working Mens' Council; his friend, Friedrich Engels, whose family had a branch of its textile business in Manchester; the German, Carl Schorlemmer, Engels' friend, who became the first British professor of organic chemistry; another German, Charles Hallé, who founded the Hallé Orchestra in Manchester; Sir Marc Isambard Brunel, the French civil engineer who was responsible for building the Rotherhithe tunnel under the Thames, and his son, Isambard Kingdom Brunel, who designed the Clifton Bridge in Bristol, and the Great Western Railway, affectionately nicknamed 'God's Wonderful Railway'; and Victor Hugo, the French novelist who wrote *Les Misérables*. All of these refugees, and many others, became actively involved in the cultural, intellectual and political life of the country. It was this philanthropic record of taking in political exiles that inspired Macaulay to dub England 'the sacred refuge of mankind'.

► One of the greatest engineers of the early Victorian age, Isambard Kingdom Brunel, was the son of French immigrants. Here he stands by the chains of his steamship, *Great Eastern*, the biggest vessel of the day, now remembered for its role in laying the first transatlantic telegraph cables.

FROM OVER THE IRISH SEA

etween the 1830s and 1850s, hundreds of thousands of Irish families fled from rural poverty and famine to make their lives elsewhere. The vast majority of Irish emigrants went to the newly independent states of America, but by 1861 a quarter of Liverpool's population was Irish-born, and Manchester, London and Glasgow had large Irish populations.

Most of the men had to take jobs that demanded exhausting physical labour. As the original 'navvies' (from 'navigators'), Irish labourers cut canals, laid railway lines and dug roads, tasks described by one historian as 'equivalent to constructing a thousand Pyramids'. They built factories and tenements, and worked in the docks and in the mines in Wales and Scotland. They also joined the army, and in 1900, for example, 15% of British regiments were made up of Irishmen. Thousands worked as casual labourers, doing odd jobs wherever they could be found. Irish women kept lodging houses, and worked as handloom weavers. In Coatbridge, a mining town in Lanarkshire, near Glasgow, the Irish proportion of the population rose from 13% in 1841 to 49% in 1851 – 60% of the metalworkers, 44% of the miners and a third of the domestic handloom weavers were Irish.

When Dr Kay conducted a survey of employers in 1835 about the value of Irish labour, he found that the English were in all 'the more ingenious and skill-requiring works' while the Irish were 'almost all to be found in the blowing rooms', with scarcely any placed in 'offices of trust'. Certain types of work were done almost entirely by the Irish, since 'the English either refused the menial, unpleasant tasks or could not keep up with the pace'.

Mid-nineteenth century Irish emigrants boarding steamers for Liverpool at Cork.

▼

DEPARTURE OF THE "NIMROD" AND "ATHLONE" STEAMERS, WITH EMIGRANTS ON BOARD, FOR LIVERPOOL.

Irish navvies built thousands of miles of British railways, roads, and canals in the nineteenth century.

Ben Tillett, the son of an Irish immigrant, organised the dockers' union and was one of the principal leaders of the successful 1889 strike against the use of contract labour. He became an MP in 1917 and president of the Trades Union Congress in 1929.

Almost everywhere, the Irish lived in the poorest houses and managed on the lowest wages, and this close acquaintance with such oppressive conditions encouraged many to become committed trade unionists and to campaign for better working conditions for everyone. John Doherty helped to organise clothing workers in Manchester in 1830; Ben Tillett, whose father was an immigrant, led the dockers in a successful strike in 1889 against the use of contract labour; Feargus O'Connor was a leading member of the Chartist Movement; and Jim Connell wrote *The Red Flag*, the song of the British labour movement, in 1889.

As citizens of the UK, the Irish were not foreigners, and while there were conflicts between Irish navvies and English, Welsh and Scottish workers, Irish labourers allowed many in the local population to escape the hardest, dirtiest and worst paid jobs. The Irish helped to build a large part of the essential infrastructure of an industrial society in Britain, and they contributed to the strengthening of trade unions at a time when there was little legal protection for employees.

The prospect of finding fame and fortune in London had long brought many Irish intellectuals, writers and artists to London. At the beginning of the eighteenth century, Jonathan Swift's talents as a pamphleteer were a gift to Tory politicians – one of his pamphlets even turned public opinion in favour of peace with France, and Dr Samuel Johnson remarked, 'For a time [Swift] dictated the political opinions of the English nation.' Another Irish immigrant, Edmund Burke, was also believed (by Matthew Arnold) to be the only man in England who 'brought thought to bear upon politics'. He was elected as an MP in 1765 and devoted his life to political causes such as the emancipation of the American colonies and Catholic emancipation.

In 1876, George Bernard Shaw arrived in London and began his literary career as a music critic – he calculated that during his nine years he earned less than £10 by his pen. He joined the Fabian Society, and gave over 1,000 lectures on women's rights, equality of income, the abolition of private property, and the simplification of English spelling and punctuation, among other subjects. By the end of his life – he died in 1950 aged 94 – he had written over 50 plays, receiving the Nobel Prize for Literature in 1925. The playwright, Oscar Wilde, was a student at Oxford when Shaw arrived. He is remembered both for his brilliant epigrammatic wit and his imprisonment for two years from 1895 to 1897 for homosexuality, which had been made a criminal offence a few years earlier. And in 1870, at 18 Stepney Causeway in London, the first Home for Destitute Boys was opened by another Irishman, Thomas Barnardo.

ESCAPING THE POGROMS

etween 1870 and 1914 about 120,000 Russian and Polish Jews fled to Britain from savage persecution. Most of them settled in London's East End, but important settlements were established in Leeds and Manchester.

The refugees could not have come at a worse time, as the country was going through its first great depression between 1873 and 1896. Unemployment was rampant, and there was no social security, only the slender provisions of the Poor Law, pawnbrokers, friendly societies, and such meagre savings as people might have. Few could spare any charity for refugees, however perilous their plight. However, the Jewish Board of Guardians set up the Poor Jews' Temporary Shelter in 1885, which provided two weeks' board and lodging to nearly all the refugees who arrived between 1895 and 1914.

Except for their faith, the refugees had little in common with Jewish people already settled in the UK. They were peasants from a relatively undeveloped part of Europe and they did not speak any English. By the end of the nineteenth century jobs in the docks were strongly unionised and were not open to them, and the casual work that was available – peddling and portering – was largely done by Irish immigrants. There were three main openings: in clothing, shoemaking and furniture, all areas of small-scale production known as sweating, because it depended on working long hours for little pay. It cost only £1 to set up as a master tailor in those days, but only a fraction of the newcomers who tried to set up businesses were successful – London was bursting with small firms. Most of the refugees started off by working for newly established Jewish clothing manufacturers, such as Montague Burton, who set up workshops in Whitechapel, Leeds and Manchester. By 1901, 40% of the Jewish refugees were tailors, 12% were in the footware trade and 10% in furniture manufacturing.

Hardly ignorant of the harsh realities of sweating, Jews set up their own clothing and furniture unions and campaigned against sweatshop conditions – in 1889, and again in 1912, 10,000 workers came out on strike for better conditions.

A campaign to curb immigration began, spearheaded by the British Brothers

Notice of a public meeting in London for Jewish men in 1876, printed in Hebrew.

A tailoring workshop in the East End of London in 1940. By 1901, 40% of the Russian Jewish refugees were tailors. Michael Marks, who arrived in 1882, was an exception. He started out as a pedlar, and opened a 'penny bazaar' shop in Manchester in 1894 with Tom Spencer, an Englishman. By 1900, Marks and Spencer had 36 outlets. Israel Sieff, the son of a Lithuanian immigrant, joined the company as a partner. Marks and Spencer is still owned by the Sieff family, and is one of Britain's premier companies today.

League. It had been set up in 1901 and was supported by a number of East End MPs such as Major Evans Gordon, Tory MP for Stepney, who moved an amendment on immigration control in the House of Commons in January 1902. In language similar to that used by Enoch Powell, MP for South West Wolverhampton, 66 years later, Gordon warned: 'A storm is brewing which, if it be allowed to burst, will have deplorable results.' In 1905, the first Aliens Act was passed to reduce the number of Jewish immigrants. Subsequent attempts by fascists to stir up anti-immigrant feeling were rebuffed by local people, most memorably at Cable Street in 1936 when thousands demonstrated against a march by Oswald Moseley's Blackshirts.

What did the Jewish refugees contribute to British society? First, they helped to develop the market for cheap clothing – the names Windsmoor, Dereta and Alexon all grew out of East End workshops. Second, the workshops they set up helped to expand employment by creating jobs in the garment trade. Third, they contributed to the development of a culture of enterprise through a keen business and commercial sense. Fourth, their own experience of working in appalling conditions led them to campaign for social justice by setting up unions and getting involved in local politics. Many of them were also largely self-reliant – by 1900 there were 186 Jewish friendly societies, as well as free schools for Jewish children. Some of these were to become well-known artists, writers, politicians and philosophers, such as the painter, Mark Gertler; the poet, Isaac Rosenberg; the playwrights, Harold Pinter and Arnold Wesker; the politicians, Phil Piratin and Emmanuel Shinwell; the mathematician, Selig Brodetsky; and the writer and Jewish spokesman, Israel Zangwill, whose play, *The Melting Pot,* gave new meaning to this phrase.

The poet, Isaac Rosenberg, who was killed in the First World War.

▼

Moses, from whose loins I sprung

Lit by a lamp in his blood

Ten immutable rules

A moon for mutable lampless men

The blond, the bronze, the ruddy

With the same heaving blood keep tide

To the moon of Moses

Then why do they sneer at me?

ISAAC ROSENBERG (1890-1918)

FOR KING AND COUNTRY

he two world wars fought during the first half of this century, between 1914 and 1918, and again between 1939 and 1945, left millions dead, wounded or homeless. During the first, or the Great War as it was known, which everyone thought would be over within a year, over six million men were mobilised in Britain's armed forces. During the second, the figure was over 4.5 million. Over a million people from the British Empire – a whole generation – were lost in the Great War, while casualties in the Second have been estimated at over three-quarters of a million.

Thousands of refugees poured into Britain during both wars – Belgians escaping from the advancing German armies in 1914; and refugees from Nazi Europe in the 1930s and 1940s. By 1943 there were 114,000 civil refugees in Britain.

Troops from the British Empire played a vital part in both wars. As British subjects, bound by allegiance to the British monarch, they were expected to fight in all Britain's wars, even wars of colonial expansion. When war was declared on Germany, for example, it was on behalf of the whole of the British Empire. Commenting on the role of the Empire in the Second World War, the historian, M R D Foot has pointed out:

Sikh infantry using bicycles to reach the front line in Flanders in the First World War. In 1882, Lord Salisbury had compared India to 'an English barracks in the Oriental Seas from which we may draw any number of troops without paying for them.' Nearly a million and a half Indian troops fought for Britain in the First World War.

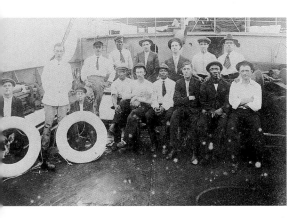

The crew of the *SS Glamorgan*, from Cardiff, just before the start of the First World War. The crews of the merchant ships which kept Britain supplied during both wars included many African, West Indian, Indian and Chinese seamen. Many went down in ships torpedoed by U-boats.

The Empire as a whole constituted a far more formidable fighting machine than the UK could ever have been alone.

We outline below some of the contributions made by people from parts of the Empire, by Polish and Czech servicemen who fought under British command during the Second World War, and by some individuals from the Empire who were resident in Britain during the wars.

WORLD WAR 1

This man in his own country prayed we know not to what Powers.
We pray them to reward him for his bravery in ours.

(Rudyard Kipling's epitaph for a Hindu sepoy in France, from *Epitaphs of the War*)

Nearly one and a half million Indians enlisted during the First World War. One estimate puts the number injured at around 107,000 and lives lost at 40,000. Indian soldiers fought in Turkey, Palestine, Mesopotamia, Egypt, Sudan, East Africa and in the trenches of the Western Front – it was the first time in imperial history that Indian troops were brought to Britain's aid in Europe. Twelve were honoured with Victoria Crosses. In addition, at its own request, India bore the expense of its own forces overseas, contributed £100 million to the war effort, raised £73 million in war loans between 1917 and 1918, and gave stores and equipment to the value of £80 million.

Men of the British West Indies Regiment fought almost everywhere and many were decorated after the war with some of the highest awards.

Sixteen servicemen from the West African Frontier Force and the King's African Rifles were awarded Distinguished Conduct Medals, while the role of Africans, as Carrier Corps, was vital in the East Africa campaign against the Germans.

Behind the front lines, the merchant marine included Africans, Asians, Chinese and West Indian seamen who kept lines of communication open, and transported food, munitions and medical supplies. Asians and Chinese – 96,000 were brought in from Shandong Province to the Western Front – formed part of the Labour Corps, who dug trenches, laid tracks and buried the dead.

In Britain itself, people of 'colonial origin' were not allowed to join the British Army. As soldiers were expected to stay with their regiments throughout their career,

Kamal Chunchie (ringed) at a military hospital in Malta in 1917. After the war, Chunchie settled in London and dedicated his life to the welfare of the 'coloured community' in the East End, first with the Methodist church, and then as pastor of the Coloured Men's Institute.

EMPIRE FORCES IN THE TWO WORLD WARS

	WWI	WW2
British Isles/UK	6,184,416	4,683,000
India	1,401,350	2,500,000
Canada	640,886	780,000
Australia	416,809	680,000
New Zealand	220,099	157,000
S Africa	136,070	140,000
Egypt		54,000

Sources: WWI: from India's Contribution to the Great War, Calcutta, 1923; WWII: from the Office of the US Army Adjutant General, cited in R Goralski, World War Two Almanac, 1931-1945.

◀ Indian troops in Italy in 1944. Two and a half million Indians fought in the Second World War, in Burma, Malaya, and North Africa, as well as in Italy.

entry was restricted to men of the same background, in order to encourage greater loyalty and a sense of belonging. At first regiments were linked to counties, such as the Royal Worcestershire Regiment, although by the middle of the war, in the wake of large casualties, these links had been broken. A few colonial residents in Britain were then accepted, such as Norman Manley, prime minister-to-be of Jamaica, then a student in Britain; Frank Dove, the Brighton-born son of a Gold Coast (now Ghana) lawyer, who fought in the Tank Corps and received the Military Medal at Cambrai in 1917; Walter Tull, a black professional footballer with Tottenham Hotspur, who died at the age of 30 on the Western Front; and Kamal Chunchie, a policeman from Ceylon, who joined the Middlesex Regiment, and was wounded twice.

WORLD WAR 2

During the Second World War, India was a supply base for Commonwealth, Chinese and US forces as well as its own troops. It provided an estimated £287 million worth of materials plus £130 million for US forces alone. Donations were made to the value of £23 million by 1943, and a further £11 million was given in interest-free war loans. It sent food, and contributed extensively to shipbuilding and repairs.

Indian soldiers fought and won the Burma campaign, and they were active on several other fronts in Malaya, North Africa, Italy and elsewhere. Indians were among the troops rescued from Dunkirk. Seventeen Indian servicemen were awarded Victoria Crosses. The Indian Women's Auxiliary Corps, which was 10,000 strong, played a wide range of non-combatant roles. The Royal Indian Navy was involved in operations and convoy work as far afield as the Mediterranean and the Atlantic, while India was also an important centre for intelligence work. The total number of Indians enrolled in all the services came to 2,500,000, the largest volunteer army in history. Casualties included 24,338 killed, over 64,000 wounded, nearly 12,000 missing and some 80,000 taken prisoner.

About 300 West Indians enlisted in the RAF for aircrew duties, and some 5,500 volunteered for ground duties. Five hundred British Honduran woodsmen were employed in the Scottish forests.

▲ Stenographers Elaine Williams and Vivien Huchoy arrived in England from Trinidad to join the Auxiliary Territorial Service in 1943.

Jamaican sappers training in England in 1941. They laid and cleared mines, built bridges, and constructed railways, airfields, and roads.

A tailgunner on an RAF bomber.

Noor Inayat Khan, secret agent 'Madeleine', was the only Asian to serve with the Special Operations Executive during the Second World War. A fluent French speaker, she operated in Paris from 1943, but was betrayed and arrested by the Gestapo. After a year in prison, she was sent to Dachau concentration camp and shot. She was posthumously awarded the *Croix de Guerre* and the George Cross.

Approximately 60,000 black people and 11,000 white people, including 1,500 women, from Northern and Southern Rhodesia and Nyasaland (now Zambia, Zimbabwe and Malawi) joined the armed forces. Many saw action in African regiments in the East African, Western Desert and Burma campaigns. The countries supplied raw materials such as copper (250,000 tons in 1943 alone), zinc and mica, which was used to produce valves for oxygen masks.

Around 100,000 men and women from British East Africa (Kenya, Uganda, Zanzibar and Tanganyika) joined the armed forces. Tanganyika (now Tanzania) supplied large quantities of rubber and sisal.

The countries of British West Africa (Nigeria, Gambia, Sierra Leone and the Gold Coast) were invaluable to the war effort. They provided troops and labourers for the West African Military Labour Corps, as well as raw materials. Freetown, the capital of Sierra Leone, was an important naval base, and the Gold Coast was the starting point for the air route to the Middle East. In the Burma campaign, 169,000 men fought as part of the West Africa Divisions – there were 2,000 casualties, including 494 dead.

Approximately one million Poles fought with the British armed services after the fall of Poland, with Generals Wladyslaw Sikorski and Wladyslaw Anders prominent in action. Polish warships escorted convoys and guarded the British coasts, and the destroyer, *Piorun*, finally sank the German warship, *Bismarck*, after a famous chase in the north Atlantic. But it was during the Battle of Britain that the Poles played an outstanding role: between 10 July and the end of October 1940, they were responsible for bringing down 203 out of 1,733 German aircraft.

A Czech armoured brigade of 5,000 men, formed in the UK, went on to serve in the

CY GRANT, the man who sang the news in calypso on BBC television after the war, joined the RAF as a navigator in Bomber Command. He was a prisoner of war in Germany for two years. He recalls his RAF days:

"I was one of the first four people who joined the RAF from the colonies. They had just changed their policy towards recruiting black people, so that's how I got in. I trained as a pilot, but then half way through my training I was switched to navigator. I didn't make anything of this at the time, because I did not realise that it was not above board. But, much later, I discovered through a friend that there were problems with the English aircrew not wanting to fly with black pilots." (Quoted in Pines, *Black and White in Colour*)

Munitions factories recruited workers from throughout the Empire during the Second World War.

Normandy campaign. Four Czech squadrons flew under the RAF. But the transfer of key members of the Czech intelligence service to London in 1939 was that country's most valuable contribution to the war effort. Polish and Czech intelligence were the first to break the German Enigma codes, which helped the British to decipher vital signals throughout the war.

About 60,000 men and women from the Irish Free State, which remained neutral during the war, crossed over to Northern Ireland or Britain and joined the British armed services. Of the 400,000 Jews in the UK, 60,000 fought in the army, 14,000 in the RAF, and 1,800 in the Royal Navy.

As in the First World War, thousands of merchant seamen including Africans, West Indians, Chinese, Asians and Somalis, kept lines of communication open, and transported supplies and food to Britain. Men from the Empire, as well as black, Asian, Irish and Jewish people in Britain, were trained for essential work in munitions factories, in various military departments, and in civil defence and army medical services.

'Never ... has so much been owed by so many to so few', was Winston Churchill's tribute to the men who fought in the Battle of Britain. Polish fighter pilots accounted for one in ten of the German aircraft shot down.

Despite an unofficial colour bar in the British army, Arundel Moody, son of Dr Harold Moody, founder of the League of Coloured Peoples in 1931, succeeded in becoming the first black British commissioned officer when he became a lieutenant in the Royal West Kent Regiment. Amelia King, a black woman from Stepney, volunteered to serve with the Women's Land Army, but was rejected because of objections from farmers. Noor Inayat Khan, was the only Asian to serve as an intelligence agent during the war. She was betrayed, and executed by the Germans at Dachau concentration camp.

FROM THE COMMONWEALTH AND FROM EUROPE

Before 1950, between 5,000 and 10,000 of the population in Britain who had been born in other countries were not white. They were largely men from the Commonwealth or Empire who had served in the war and decided not to return home, although there were also some students, seamen and a few professionals. As British subjects they were entitled to live here.

The whole of Europe was occupied with the massive task of reconstruction after the war, and there were labour shortages everywhere. In Britain, more hands were needed in agriculture and forestry, transport, engineering, mining, textile work, brick manufacture, foundries, construction, and the new national health service. The school-leaving age had been raised, and women who had worked in factories during the war were encouraged to return to being housewives and mothers. Thousands of people emigrated to Canada, Australia, South Africa and New Zealand – a net loss to the population of some 64,000 people in 1953 alone. Britain has usually been a country of net emigration, but this was still high.

The government positively encouraged immigration. Initially, as the government's *Economic Review* in 1947 showed, Europe was viewed as the 'only substantial additional source of manpower'. The 100,000 (former) members of the Polish armed forces under British command, and their families, who did not want to return to a newly communist Poland formed the largest refugee group in Britain after the war. Most settled in London, Lancashire and Yorkshire, and received substantial help from the government to make the transition to civilian life.

Two other immigrant groups came to Britain under the European Volunteer Workers scheme set up immediately after the war. One was the displaced persons, casualties of the war living in refugee camps all over Europe – 85,000 Ukrainians, Yugoslavs, Estonians, Latvians and Lithuanians came to Britain under various resettlement schemes between 1946 and 1950. The other group included people from the continent brought in to work in specific sectors where there were shortages.

It soon became clear to the government, however, that many more workers would be needed if the recovery was not to slow down – even in 1956 there were 174,000 more unfilled vacancies than unemployed workers – so active recruitment began in Ireland, in the colonies

By 1954, when this picture was taken at Southampton, around 10,000 West Indians, mostly from Jamaica, had responded to the British Government's recruitment drive in the Caribbean. ▼

and in countries of the New Commonwealth, the term used to describe the countries that were becoming independent as the Empire was gradually dismantled. Australia, Canada, New Zealand and South Africa made up the Old Commonwealth. Irish immigration only increased after 1951, however, when there was a slump in the Irish economy. By the end of the 1960s there were 900,000 Irish-born immigrants in Britain – and they are still the largest immigrant group in Britain.

In June 1948, the *SS Empire Windrush* brought the first 492 Jamaican immigrants to Tilbury, many of whom had served in the RAF during the war. The London Transport Executive helped thousands of Barbadians and Trinidadians with loans for fares, and the British Hotels and Restaurants Association set up recruitment offices in Jamaica. However, West Indians began arriving in numbers only in the 1950s when immigration to the USA became difficult. The vast majority – 90% – came to the UK to find work, and had not considered settling here permanently.

Immigration from India and Pakistan began later, and peaked in the 1960s. Punjabi Sikhs were among the first to arrive, partly because of the dislocations caused by the partition of India in 1947, and partly because of their long history of migration in the service of the Empire and in both World Wars. Some Pakistanis came from east Pakistan, traditionally a land of emigration. When East Pakistan declared its independence in 1971, it became known as Bangladesh. Several Australians, Iranians, Iraqis, Egyptians, Palestinians and Sudanese also arrived during the 1950s and 1960s. Both the Chinese and Greek-Cypriot populations in Britain also grew during the 1960s.

Pressure for immigration control mounted in Britain. Rumours that the government was planning to restrict entry led to more people trying to get in before the ban, and this in turn fuelled the demands for control. The Commonwealth Immigrants Act was passed in 1962, and introduced an employment voucher system restricting entry to skilled and professional people.

In 1968, a new Commonwealth Immigrants Act denied British nationals in East African countries the right to enter Britain. Immigration from the New Commonwealth, already restricted by a series of legislative measures from 1962 onwards, was virtually ended by the Immigration Act of 1971, except for reasons of family reunion – and even this was exceedingly difficult in practice. However, the Act's definition of 'patriality' – having a parent or grandparent born in the UK – allowed some millions of Old Commonwealth citizens to settle in Britain if they chose.

The 1960s and 1970s brought refugees from Kenya, Uganda, and Malawi. Some of them were descendants of Gujaratis who had originally gone to Africa from India as contract workers, while others had migrated from India as traders. There were also some Parsis, and Catholics from Goa. At the time when Britain's 1968 Act blocked entry to Britain for most of them, the people of Indian origin in East Africa included many professionals and civil servants as well as business people. Kenya's 'Africanisation' policy, Idi Amin's expulsion of Asians from Uganda, and Hastings Banda's similar threats in Malawi left African Asians with no choice but to come here – they had British passports. Britain asked the world to 'share the burden' of these British refugees, most of whom had invaluable professional and business skills. Canada jumped in and welcomed 10,000 applicants – it was an opportunity to get

Searching for accommodation in Notting Hill Gate in 1955. The new immigrants often found that the hands of friendship extended during the war were quickly withdrawn once they came to Britain to fill vacant jobs and find a home.

Calypso, which immigrants from Trinidad brought with them, had achieved wide popularity in Britain by the mid 1950s.

British Asians arriving at Stansted airport in 1972 after being expelled from Uganda by Idi Amin.

highly professional skills that another country had paid to develop – while Britain accepted 27,000 refugees over several years.

By the end of the 1970s, immigration from the New Commonwealth was already under strict control, yet a new British Nationality Act was passed in 1981 'to reduce future sources of primary immigration'. Under its provisions, British citizenship ceased to be an automatic right if one was born in Britain, and became conditional upon the citizenship of one's parents. There are now five types of British citizenship.

Refugees have been admitted to Britain since the end of the war from various countries including Hungary, Chile, Cyprus, Argentina, Somalia, Lebanon, Sudan, Iran, Sri Lanka, Vietnam, Nigeria, Turkey, Iraq and, most recently, from former Yugoslavia. Many refugees have qualifications and professional skills. According to a Home Office study, nearly half have some sort of higher or further education, and over a third have a degree, compared with 12% of British adults – but most are not allowed to work in this country. A new panic about illegal asylum-seekers has led to a series of restrictive legal measures to deter applicants. The contrast with the Victorians' liberal approach to accepting political refugees could not be greater.

The majority of primary immigrants to Britain today come from three groups: citizens of the member states of the European Union, who now have the status of internal migrants; citizens of the Republic of Ireland; and work permit holders, mainly from the USA and Japan. In 1992, work permit holders who had lived in the UK for four years made up the largest category of applicants accepted for settlement.

RACE RELATIONS

This book is not the place to explore the very complex history of race relations in Britain, but there can be no true appreciation of the contributions made by post-war immigrants to the culture and society we take so much for granted today without some awareness of their initial reception and the distance they have had to travel to win recognition of their right to participate fully in British society, as equal citizens. Mr Fairweather, a much decorated black serviceman in the Second World War, compared the magnificent hospitality which he had received in 1943 with the attitudes he encountered when he returned to Britain after being demobbed in Jamaica:

> Things had changed. They hated the very sight of you once it was over. But I say, if I am good enough to die in your wars, then I am good enough to live with you.

The new West Indian and Asian immigrants often received a cool welcome, and signs in pubs and lodging house windows made it clear that, however much the British economy might need them, some British people thought otherwise. Just as Bermondsey had been dubbed Petty Burgundy four hundred years before, streets in the Midlands, London and the North West were referred to as Little Jamaica or Little Punjab.

The familiar complaints about 'foreigners', which immigrants throughout history have had to contend with, were also levelled at the latest arrivals. They were accused of taking jobs from local British people, even though they had only come to Britain because of labour shortages. It was believed that they were a burden to the country, although a study by a British economist in 1966 showed that the total amount spent on social welfare for an immigrant then was £49 compared to an average of £62 for every person in Britain. Immigrants past and present have had to stand up to such unfounded claims. But black people, Asians, Chinese and other 'non-white' ethnic minorities have had to contend with racial prejudice as well; for example only 17% of white people in Birmingham in 1956 thought 'coloured people' were equal to them, and when Enoch Powell, MP for South West Wolverhampton, called for the repatriation of 'coloured' immigrants in 1969, his popularity rose.

But there were millions who rejected his views, and hundreds of thousands who have been actively involved in the campaigns mounted over the years against racial discrimination and inequality. In 1976, a new, stronger Race Relations Act was passed, and the Commission for Racial Equality was set up to work for a just society free of racial discrimination. Today, twenty years later, racial equality is one of the most important issues for young people in Britain. They have grown up in a multi-ethnic and racially diverse society, and know no other.

WE AND THEY

Father, Mother and Me

Sister and Auntie say

All the people like us are We,

And every one else is They.

And They live over the sea,

While we live over the way,

But – would you believe it? –

They look upon We

As only a sort of They?

RUDYARD KIPLING

◀

The biggest and most famous street festival in Europe, Notting Hill Carnival has been the scene of racial tension in the past. By the time this picture was taken, in the early 1990s, it had become a symbol, and celebration, of a diverse Britain, attracting hundreds of thousands of people from all ethnic groups every year.

II

THE CONTRIBUTIONS
OF BRITAIN'S
ETHNIC
MINORITIES

THE ETHNIC COMPOSITION OF BRITAIN'S POPULATION, FROM THE 1991 CENSUS

Ethnic group	No.	%
White	51,873,794	94.5
Black Caribbean	499,964	0.9
Black African	212,362	0.4
Black – other	178,401	0.3
Indian	840,255	1.5
Pakistani	476,555	0.9
Bangladeshi	162,835	0.3
Chinese	156,938	0.3
Other Asian	197,534	0.4
Other – other	290,206	0.5
Total ethnic minority population	**3,015,051**	**5.5**
Black ethnic groups	890,727	1.6
South Asian	1,479,645	2.7
Chinese and others	644,678	1.2

PEOPLE BORN OUTSIDE GREAT BRITAIN AND RESIDENT HERE, FROM THE 1991 CENSUS

Countries of birth	As percentage of Great Britain's population	Number living in Great Britain
Ireland	1.5%	837,500
Other European Community	0.9%	493,900
Scandinavia and EFTA	0.1%	58,300
Eastern Europe and (then) USSR	0.3%	↑42,900
Near and Middle East	0.2%	128,300
Old Commonwealth (Aust, NZ, Canada)	0.3%	177,400
New Commonwealth	3.1%	1,688,400
Caribbean	0.5%	264,600
South Asia	1.4%	787,500
South East Asia	0.3%	150,400
East Africa	0.4%	220,600
West and southern Africa	0.2%	110,700
Rest of the world	1.0%	566,200
Asia	0.4%	231,000
North Africa	0.1%	44,600
Rest of Africa and South Africa	0.2%	102,300
The Americas	0.3%	185,000
Total born outside Great Britain	7.3%	3,991,000

ETHNIC DIVERSITY IN BRITAIN TODAY

A t the 1991 census, there were 3,015,050 people living in Britain who were not white, 5.5% of the whole population. Nearly half of them lived in Greater London, while the rest were concentrated in the Midlands, the South East and the North West of England, and Yorkshire and Humberside. Nearly three-quarters of them lived in the metropolitan counties compared with just under a third of the population overall. Four million people (7.3%) were born outside the UK, including 245,000 born in Northern Ireland. The largest groups were Irish people born in the Irish Republic (592,000) and Indians (409,000). There were about 54 groups of 10,000 or more people who were born in other countries. Of the population born outside Britain, 61% were white.

▲

A diverse group of youngsters waiting for their *paan*, an Indian version of chewing gum.

People from ethnic minorities, like the rest of the population, work in all sectors of the economy – the private and public sectors, manufacturing and services. When post-war immigrants arrived in Britain, the vacancies they helped to fill were concentrated in particular industries such as manufacturing, transport, health, hotels and restaurants. Since the 1980s, opportunities have increased, and access to jobs is gradually becoming more open. In many sectors, people from ethnic minorities can be found carrying high responsibility. However, that is not to say that all occupations and professions are equally open, or that racial discrimination is no longer an obstacle; far from it. There is still only one Asian Assistant Chief Constable in the country – Tarique Ghaffur in Lancashire; there are no judges above circuit level from the non-white ethnic minorities; only 1.4% of all members of the armed services, and 2% of the appointees to public bodies in Britain, are from non-white ethnic minorities; and unemployment rates are twice as high for ethnic minority groups as for the population as a whole. The continuing concentration of people from particular ethnic minorities in certain industries, and in the lower grades, while leaving little doubt of their vital role in these areas, is equally a sign that the labour market is far from free of racial discrimination and disadvantage.

The following sections focus on those areas where post-war immigrants and their descendants have made the most striking contributions since they settled in Britain.

As this section refers to data collected at the 1991 census and by Labour Force Surveys, we have roughly followed the ethnic classifications used in the census. The term 'Asian' refers to people from, or with origins in, the countries of the Indian subcontinent. The term 'black' refers to people from, or with origins in, Africa and the Caribbean. Wherever possible, however, we have tried to give more specific details about the ethnic group in question. It is important to note that the census data on 'ethnic minorities' do not include Britain's white ethnic minorities, wherever they were born. As used by the census and the Labour Force Survey, the term 'ethnic minority' therefore includes all those who do not identify themselves as 'white'.

INDUSTRY AND ENTERPRISE

F or the first 25 years after the Second World War, unemployment never rose above 2%. There was always work to be done, and a report by the Department of Employment in 1976 confirmed that, although immigrants, including workers born in the Irish Republic, made up only 6% of working people in Britain, they still formed a 'sizeable element in the labour force of some firms and industries,' such as transport and communications, health, textiles, food manufacturing, hotels and catering, and metal manufacturing.

From 1947 to 1976, at the London Brick Company's Stewartby works near Bedford, then the largest brick works in the world, 30-40% of the workforce were born overseas. It included Poles, Italians, Indians, Pakistanis and West Indians. Poles

also worked on farms and in the mines, and Italians in the steel works in South Wales. It was largely Irish workers who built the new motorways, and the tower blocks and industrial units rising out of the rubble of the war-time blitz. They were also involved in such major civil engineering projects as the Festival of Britain. To this day, the green J Murphy trucks in London's streets, the 'Brown Macs' of McNicholas Engineering and Alfred McAlpine 's civil engineering workers remind us that the Irish have a long history of work in the construction industry. In 1991, 32% of people born in the Irish Republic and living in Britain were construction workers. Black people were more likely than any other non-white minority group to go into the building trade. The Alfred McAlpine Group has recently gone into partnership with a new black construction company set up by Chris Shokoya-Eleshin in 1992 to employ local people to build social housing in Liverpool. Forty-one homes have already been built as part of a £2.5 million inner city development project in Liverpool on behalf of the Steve Biko Housing Association.

Many of the West Indians and Asians who found jobs in the manufacturing sector during the 1950s and 1960s were well educated, sometimes up to and beyond undergraduate degree level, but they were often only able to secure semi-skilled or unskilled work. The new immigrants found jobs in electrical engineering factories, food and drink plants, car manufacturing plants, car components firms, clothing and footwear companies, foundries, paper mills, and rubber and plastic works.

At the United Biscuits factory in Harlesden, north-west London, 80% of

▲
Ukrainian 'displaced persons' picking potatoes in South Wales in 1948.

Gino Pedroni, one of 1,500 Italians recruited to work in British coal mines in 1952, talks to the manager at Norton Hill colliery before starting his shift.
▼

▲
Signposts of a new era: in some rural areas, workers from Italy were so numerous that road signs were put up in Italian.

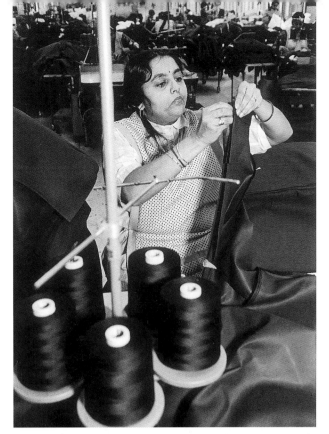

workers on the production line were black or Asian; and at Coneygre foundry in Tipton 70% of the 500 workers were Asian. In the textile industries, where the costs of mechanisation could be borne only by keeping the machines going all the time, Indian and Pakistani men worked night shifts, which the predominantly female workforce were not allowed to do. The result was a racially segregated workforce. In many mills in West Yorkshire, 50-80% of the workers were Asian. Jobs in some traditional, strongly unionised industries such as the docks and printing were closed to the new immigrants, as they had been to Jewish refugees at the turn of the century.

A textile millworker in Bradford. In 1961, 70,000 people were working in Bradford's textile mills, and many were Pakistani immigrants. Today, there are 9,600 millworkers. Unemployment in Bradford's Pakistani community stands at about 36%, compared to an average for the city of about 9%.

The huge demand for cars and consumer goods such as refrigerators, vacuum cleaners, radios, and TVs generated constant pressure to increase factory output. Many workers quit as the conditions in factories and plants worsened. The labour manager of Edge Tools Ltd recalled: 'We tried employing continentals and refugees but it didn't work out ... in 1950 [we] employed Indian workers.' Ford in Dagenham, London, had the same problem; conditions were so gruelling that anyone who could find a decent job elsewhere left. Thus, black and Asian workers came to form the majority of the Dagenham workforce. Even in 1984, nearly 38% of hourly-paid workers at Dagenham were black and Asian and, according to one estimate, they made up 70% of the workers in the assembly plant and 50% in the body and engine plants. Only among foremen and in the export department was there a majority of white workers.

With essential industries depending heavily on the new immigrants' labour, the newcomers were undeniably an integral part of the British economy. *The Times* was right on the two occasions when it tried to explain to its readers how indispensable immigrant labour was to Britain. Writing about the impact of European workers on 22 May 1951, the paper said:

> The result can be measured directly in terms of more food for the workers, more coal for vital industries, more cloth for export, more bricks for housing.

Nearly fifteen years later, on 27 January 1965, the headline ran, *Life would be worse for us without coloured workers*, and explained:

> ...Britain could not live as it does ... London Transport would be disrupted ... Bus services in several of our major cities would suffer badly. Important sections of industry in the Midlands would slow down. The shortage of bricks would worsen. Lunches would be harder to get in London's cafes; streets in some cities would become filthy. Life in Britain for many people who criticise coloured immigrants most would be harder and more unpleasant without them.

Between 1960 and 1981, London and the other industrial conurbations lost 1.7 million manufacturing jobs, 79% of the 2.1 million jobs lost across the nation as a

Raj Bagri was 15 when he became an apprentice in the metal trade in Calcutta. He moved to London in 1959, and set up his own company, Metdist, in 1970. It is now one of the largest privately held businesses in the UK, and its annual turnover is over £700 million. Raj Bagri became the first person of non-British origin to be appointed Chairman of the Metal Exchange in 1993, and has been re-elected three times. Under Bagri's chairmanship, London metal exchange turnovers have increased sevenfold in recent years, and the market now contributes approximately $US250 million a year to the UK balance of payments. Bagri was awarded a CBE for his services to the metal manufacturing industry.

38% of hourly paid workers at Ford's Dagenham plant in 1984 were Asian or black.

Mr Habib Ullah in one of his two Stornoway clothes shops. He came to the Isle of Lewis from a small village in Pakistan, and started out as a travelling salesman, taking his woollen cardigans, jumpers and scarves all over the island.

whole. Unemployment increased by 138% between 1972 and 1981, but for black and Asian workers, who were heavily employed in manufacturing, it went up by 325%. The jobs in the new hotels, warehouses and supermarkets, and in the expanding 'service sector' – in banks, building societies, insurance companies, local government and public services – were insufficient to absorb those who were without work. Moreover, many of the jobs were part-time.

Some ethnic minority workers who had lost their jobs used their redundancy money, topped up sometimes with help from their families, and in some cases bank loans, to set up their own businesses. In 1991, 25% of working Indian men, 27% of working Pakistani men and 33% of working Chinese men in Britain were self-employed compared with 18% of the overall working population. In Scotland the figures were much higher – 38%, 54% and 37% respectively compared with 14% overall, and the figures for Wales were also high. The increase since 1974, when only 8% of working Asians were self-employed compared with 12% overall, is striking.

The census also revealed that about 10% of Indian and Pakistani self-employed men, and 20% of Chinese self-employed men created jobs for other people compared with 6% of self-employed men overall. In Wales and Scotland, the figures were much higher, with 32% of self-employed Pakistani men and 28% of self-employed Chinese men in Scotland, for example, employing others, compared with 6% overall. Chinese and Pakistani women were far more likely to be self-employed than any other group, and to employ others, especially in Scotland and Wales. Regional surveys also show that in some areas up to 55% of Jewish people may be self-employed.

In Leicester, a study commissioned by the City Council in 1994 found that 1,446 companies were owned by Asians, representing 1 in 6 of all Leicester businesses. They provided 8% of all the jobs in the city. It seems that Ugandan Asian women have been equally, if not more, enterprising. A study by the University of Wales in Swansea showed that, while 25% of Ugandan Asian men were doing managerial work in 1981, by 1991 that had risen to 37%. Ugandan Asian women in managerial positions showed an increase from 6% to 24% over the same period, while the proportion of white men in managerial positions rose from 23% to 28%.

Around three-quarters of all small businesses were set up after 1980. A quick glance at any trade directory will show how rapidly ethnic minority businesses have expanded. The world of small business has always been a tough one, and most businesses stay small. But some have grown spectacularly into multi-million pound concerns. Yaqub Ali, who arrived in Hamilton, Scotland, in 1980, barely speaking any English, and with little money to his name, was awarded an OBE for his services to trade and industry in 1984 and received the Aims of Industry award in 1991. His wholesale grocery and liquor business employed 448 staff that year and had a turnover of nearly £99 million. Nathu Puri arrived in 1966 and started working as a trainee engineer with F G Skerritt, the construction company. In the mid-1970s, he set up as a consultant engineer and bought the company out when it ran into difficulties. He also established his own firm, Melton Medes, which has interests in engineering, paper, textiles and plastics. Swraj Paul's Caparo Industries now has an annual turnover of £350 million; Raj Bagri's Metdist is one of the largest privately held businesses in the UK – and he is the first person of non-British origin to have been appointed Chairman of the Metal Exchange, three times in a row. Jim Brathwaite's EMG multi-media computer

THE TIMES WEDNESDAY JANUARY 27 1965

The Dark
Million—9

LIFE WOULD BE HARDER FOR ALL OF
US WITHOUT COLOURED LABOUR

In many mills the night shift is composed almost entirely of Pakistanis. Immigrants play a vital part in running hospitals, bus services, brickworks, cafés. . . . But jobs are sometimes denied them because of white workers' hostility.

From Our Special Correspondent

29 January
1965, *The Times*

◄

Jim Brathwaite's Brighton-based Epic Multimedia Group has been valued at £20 million on the alternative stock market. EMG writes programs on CD-rom and supplies interactive programs to customers such as NatWest and British Telecom. It also produces games and educational programs. Brathwaite was born in Barbados in 1953, and worked as an accountant at Beecham Pharmaceuticals before setting up his own business.

Forty-five year old Sudhir Junanker is Associate Director of Economic Analysis in the Economics Directorate of the Confederation of British Industry, a position he was appointed to in February 1994. He is responsible for undertaking the CBI's business surveys, editing the *Economic Situation Report*, and producing the organisation's quarterly forecasts of the UK economy. He is also a member of the Industrial Prospects Group run by the chief economic adviser to the Chancellor of the Exchequer.

A Maharashtrian, Junankar came to England as a schoolboy from New Delhi, where he was born. He trained as an economist at the London School of Economics and joined the CBI in 1987, becoming a Fellow of the Royal Society of Arts in 1995.

"Visibility is an important element in changing attitudes. The first thing people from the Indian subcontinent think when they see me on TV is that it is unusual to see an Indian face in a mainstream position. This has a positive effect – people see that it can be done, that things can change, even though there are obstacles.

"Many people from the UK find themselves at a disadvantage in Europe, partly because of language. But my experience of diversity in India, a big country with lots of languages, gives me a greater facility for dealing with people of different cultures. In India everything is different, in the north from in the south, for example, which is the equivalent of that found by people in England when they go to Moscow. Going to different parts of Europe is less of a change for me because I am more used to that difference. I am more aware of how people react, how they behave in meetings, and of non-verbal communication. It is unusual in Europe for people to see someone of Indian origin representing the UK."

publishing business has just been floated on the Alternative Stock Exchange; Wing Yip says four food warehouses are only the beginning as far as he is concerned; the Okhai family, which rescued the 200-year-old Dundee firm, James Keiller Marmalade, has moved into soft drinks and packaging; Tom Singh's New Look Ltd clothes chain was sold in 1995 for £170 million; Vipin and Anant Shah's Meghraj Bank, set up in 1972 to channel the savings of the immigrant community towards its entrepreneurs, has been diversifying recently into merchant banking, insurance broking and property consultancy; and Mohammed Anwar Perwez, founder of Bestway Group of cash and carry stores, has been awarded an OBE.

Immigrants who had settled in Britain before the war included thousands of Jewish refugees, some of whom set up businesses. The economic conditions in Britain were very different when they began their careers. In 1946, Thorn Electrical Industries, the firm established by Sir Jules Thorn, an Austrian Jewish refugee to Britain between the wars, was still fairly small, and made electrical lamps and fluorescent tubes. It grew by acquiring radio businesses, such as Fergusons, and by diversifying into other sectors. Another refugee, Chaim Schreiber, was an architect whose first job in Britain involved working on Mosquito aircraft. After the war he went into cabinet-making for radio and TV sets, and then into furniture. By 1938, Jewish refugees had started 250 businesses and created 15-25,000 jobs, many in the clothing sector, but also in technical industries.

Sir Charles Clore, the son of a Jewish immigrant textile manufacturer, attracted attention in 1953 when he took over the long-established footwear manufacturing and retail business, J Sears and Co (formerly Freeman, Hardy and Willis). When he died in 1979, Clore's numerous companies employed 50,000 people and had a turnover of £1,000 million. Many other household names such as Lord Arnold Weinstock's General Electric Company, Sir John Cohen's Tesco stores, Cyril Stein's Ladbroke Group, Sir Stanley Kalms's Dixons, Alan Sugar's Amstrad, and Gerald Ratner's jewellery group have followed this route.

The success of ethnic minority entrepreneurs has often been accompanied by community and social concern; for example Godfrey Bradman's Rosehaugh Group, which is involved in the King's Cross redevelopment scheme, among others, has supported the Freedom of Information campaign and Friends of the Earth, as well as underwriting the legal costs of 1,500 people claiming damages against the manufacturers of Opren, a drug for arthritis sufferers; while Swraj Paul has donated £1 million to the children's zoo in Regent's Park, London.

▲

Swraj Paul came to Britain in the mid-1960s. His company, Caparo Industries, manufactures steel and engineering products and has an annual turnover of £350 million. He is a Fellow of the Royal Society of Arts and a Governor of Thames Valley University. In 1993, he made a gift of £1 million towards the redevelopment of the children's zoo at Regent's Park in memory of his daughter, who died of leukaemia.

TEXTILES AND CLOTHING

In Manchester, a new textile industry has recently grown out of the ashes of the old one, which had been steadily declining since the beginning of the century. Pakistani families take most of the credit for this.

Their involvement in the trade began at the turn of the century when Asian lascars found that they could scrape together a living as pedlars selling clothes and trinkets. They could be seen dragging their suitcases through the city in all weathers, selling hosiery, woollens and knitwear from door to door. In time they graduated to selling from street market stalls, before some went on to become small-scale chain retailers. The most successful were eventually able to begin buying out the old Jewish manufacturing and wholesale firms.

Their factories no longer produce the old workers' cloth caps or raincoats, but casual wear, trousers, jeans, skirts and coordinates. They also supply the mail order catalogue firms in Yorkshire and the north west. Shami Ahmed's Joe Bloggs jeans company is one of the most successful of these Manchester firms.

Similarly, a brand new clothing industry has grown up in Birmingham. Sikhs are the driving force behind it, producing raincoats and anoraks. Asians in Leicester manufacture knitwear, and in London Cypriots, Bangladeshis and Pakistanis now do the work in Tower Hamlets, Hackney and Haringey that the Jewish refugees once did in the East End, still making dresses, blouses and fashion wear. Producing garments in small batches is still the most effective way of keeping up with rapid changes in fashion, and much of the work continues to be done by women at home, whose rates of pay are set in competition with cheap imports.

▲
A homeworker in Coventry.

The widest jeans in the world from Shami Ahmed's Manchester-based Joe Bloggs. Ahmed came to Britain from Pakistan when he was two, and launched Joe Bloggs in 1986. It is now an international concern.
▼

FOOD MANUFACTURING

When the large multinational food companies began shedding jobs in the 1970s, some of the workers set up their own businesses. The new taste for 'foreign' foods, cultivated by the boom in restaurants, and by the swelling tourist industry, coincided neatly with the competition between big retail outlets to sell their own brands, and the growth in contract catering. In 1981, 12% of employees in London's food industry were working in the 'ethnic' food sector, the third largest after brewing and baking.

Dounne Alexander started from her council house kitchen where she made her Gramma's Hot Pepper Sauces. She now has a factory in Essex and 650 outlets. Department stores such as Fortnum and Mason and Harrods sell her sauces, and Alexander has won the Women Mean Business Award.

Pataks, which began life as a samosa shop in Euston, London, when Kirit and Meena Patak came to Britain from Kenya, was the fastest growing brand in Britain in 1993, with a 92% increase in retail sales.

Gulam Noon, who was born in India, set up a British branch of Bombay Halwa Royal Sweets, an Indian confectionery company, in 1970. There are now 45 outlets around the country. Noon Products, his own company, which was set up in 1988 and has 200 staff, is a multi-million pound concern. Its frozen, pre-cooked Indian meals are made for Bird's Eye and sold by Sainsbury, Waitrose, and Trust House Forte Welcome Break restaurants, and are served on 40 British Airways flights every week.

▶

Perween Warsi came to Britain from India in 1975. She started by supplying snacks to local pubs and restaurants, before setting up S&A Foods in Derby. In 1986, she won contracts to supply Asda and Safeway with S&A Foods' own Shahi brand of ready-to-cook chilled meals. In 1994, the *Independent on Sunday* reported that S&A Foods was the fifth fastest growing private company in Britain, with a £20 million turnover and 350 employees. In 1996, S&A Foods, with TV chef Ken Hom, launched a new range of dishes. Perween Warsi was the Midlands Businesswoman of the Year in 1994. Her ambition is to make S&A Foods the first British multinational to be run by a woman.

RETAIL AND BUSINESS SERVICES

lthough the big increase in independent business and retail services came after the job losses of the 1970s, some immigrants had set up shops shortly after they arrived in Britain. Unable to find the ingredients they needed for their food, they began selling halal meat and importing foodstuffs. Tilda, whose rice can now be bought in supermarkets, was among the pioneers. In Bradford, the number of Pakistani grocers and butchers rose from two in 1959 to 51 in 1967. As their communities grew, so did the demand for services such as mortgage advice, travel arrangements, entertainment, and even banking facilities, and the entrepreneurs among them were quick to take advantage. By 1965, there were 105 immigrant-owned commercial and business premises in Bradford, ranging from furniture dealers to car-hire firms. And by the late 1960s, Asians had bought up 200 cinema houses which were being closed down or demolished, in places like Manchester, Gravesend and Glasgow, and were using them to show imported Hindi films. The business was worth £1.5 million a year.

Self-employment grew by over a million in the 1980s. Some ethnic minority businesses specialise in products and services for their own communities, such as saris or black hair and beauty products. Others concentrate on a particular sector because of traditional skills or the networks they have developed. Most, though, because of financial constraints, have been obliged to start off in low-cost services such as minicab firms or local shops, in order to get their foot on the ladder.

▲

Perhaps the most famous shop in Britain, Harrods has been owned since 1985 by Egyptian-born Mohamed Al Fayed, Chairman of House of Fraser Holdings. He is seen here tossing pizza bases at the opening of a new pizzeria at the store in 1995. He and his brother had just won leave to obtain a judicial review of a Home Office decision to refuse them British citizenship.

◄

Wing Yip came to Britain 36 years ago from Hong Kong. He started life as a waiter on a basic wage of £4 and now owns four food warehouses in London, Birmingham and Manchester with a turnover of £55 million, importing 2,500 product lines. When asked to explain his success, Wing Yip said: 'I am not a good businessman, it's just that others are worse.'

▶

Mr and Mrs Misra in Brighton run one of
Britain's many small local shops.

Juda and Metka Fiszer are Polish Jews who
came to London at the beginning of this
century. They opened their umbrella shop in
Hackney in 1907.
▼

LOCAL SHOPS

Corner shops, which used to be the anchor of working class life in Britain, suffered their first blow in the early part of this century when chain stores such as Woolworths and Boots took away many of their customers. The growth of giant supermarkets such as Tesco, Asda and Sainsbury was even more damaging, and many proprietors began selling up, unable to compete any longer. Between 1973 and 1981, 11,000 independent retail shops folded, especially in the inner cities. Yet Asians, many from East Africa, were buying them and running them successfully – Charles Patel's company, Vapgate, for example, grew from one shop in 1975 to 300 in 1992.

On 12 January 1992, the *Independent on Sunday* reported that out of a total of 46,000 confectionery, tobacco and newspaper shops, an estimated 30,000 were owned by Asians. And out of 83,200 independently owned neighbourhood shops in the UK, 70% were owned by Asians. The secret of their success is flexibility, and the ability to stay one step ahead of their competitors. The shops stay open late as well as on Sundays, some develop specialist lines, and many now serve as outlets for lottery tickets. The value of the facility they provide in inner cities is incalculable, especially for elderly people, the young, the unemployed, and those who do not have cars.

▶

Tottenham Court Road is
London's hi-fi and computer land. A salesman from Micro Anvika Computers is
surrounded by his software.

48

PERSONAL PRODUCTS

Until the 1960s the black population in Britain was too small to make it worthwhile for companies to cater specifically for their needs. Black women in Britain often had to make do with cosmetics and hair products developed for different complexions and aesthetic tastes. Some even asked family and friends in the USA to mail them suitable products. So when Dudley Dryden and Len Dyke set up in business in 1967 – later to be joined by Tony Wade – to sell records and black beauty products, they were developing a new branch of the industry. Dyke and Dryden is now a multi-million pound supplier of black hair and beauty products for the British and export markets, selling to 15 countries and employing 30 staff. Rona Stephens is another one who has taken advantage of the growing market, and her Koca Karmel products are now sold through several West End department stores in London as well as through pharmacies all over the country.

The market for black hair care and cosmetics in Britain today is worth about £30 million a year, with black people spending on average between three to five times the amount spent by the population as a whole on all types of cosmetics.

Anita Roddick, the daughter of Italian immigrants to Britain, and her husband Gordon, created another opportunity in the personal products industry. With public concern mounting about the scale and cruelty of animal testing, as well as fears about toxic chemicals, the Roddicks launched the Body Shop in Brighton in 1976 with 25 natural products based on ingredients from developing countries. Twenty years later they have 1,399 outlets and 10,000 employees world-wide.

▲
Len Dyke (left) and Dudley Dryden (right) who set up Dyke and Dryden. Here they are with Britain's world heavyweight boxing champion, Lennox Lewis, who was brought up in Canada.

COMMERCE AND BANKING

Almost all the new immigrant communities got involved sooner or later in importing goods that were unavailable in Britain from their home countries: spices, curry pastes, olives, lentils, soya beans, saris, black hair products, films, videos, records, and books. Antony Chatwell runs the firm his father set up in 1931 as Bombay Emporium to sell Chinese and Indian condiments to ex-India army and civil service personnel. BE International is now a large import and export business supplying supermarkets with Lotus products, Amoy sauces and Rajah condiments.

Evidence of the growth of economic activity as a result of the presence of some of Britain's new settler communities comes from figures giving the number of business trips made by Indians to Britain: 47,000 business trips were made in 1994 compared with 13,000 in 1977 – a 262% increase. By comparison, the rate of increase in

▶

Staff at Midland Bank.
In 1991, 14% of Black Africans,
11% of Black Caribbeans and 11% of
Indians were working in financial and
business services compared with an
overall average of 12%.

Vipin and Anant Shah's
Meghraj Bank was set up in
1972. It has recently been
diversifying into merchant
banking, insurance broking
and property consultancy.

business trips by South Africans and Australians over the same period was 104% and 96% respectively.

As immigrants became settlers, those who turned to business as a way of making their livelihoods sometimes found it easier to borrow money from foreign banks or British ethnic minority-run banks, such as Meghraj Bank. Some ethnic minority entrepreneurs have complained of lack of sympathy or understanding by the high street banks, or what are considered onerous collateral requirements. The availability of credit has often been a central difficulty for small businesses. Three factors are beginning to make a difference in the attitudes of British clearing banks to the specific needs of ethnic minority businesses: the developing culture of enterprise in Britain; growing recognition that the estimated £2 billion that Asians alone are believed to invest in the British economy is probably not far off the mark; and greater awareness that equality of opportunity is good for business, leading to a gradual increase in the number of ethnic minority employees in the financial and banking sector. In 1991, 14% of Black Africans, 11% of Black Caribbeans and 11% of Indians were working in financial and business services, both as employees and as independent operators, compared with 12% of the working population overall.

TRAVEL AGENCIES

With families planning regular holidays back to their countries of origin, travel agencies became a growing area of ethnic minority enterprise. Entrepreneurs in the new immigrant communities developed good contacts with the airlines that had flights to their countries, and tracked down the cheapest fares. Everton Forbes, for example, was among the first to organise charter flights to the Caribbean in 1968. The services these agencies now offer through 'bucket' shops find buyers from all ethnic groups as well as holidaymakers more generally. Preliminary analysis of the 1992/3 Labour Force Survey shows that 13% of employees in British travel agencies were born abroad.

TRANSPORT

The years between 1950 and 1980 were difficult ones for London Transport. In 1974, for example, the number of unfilled vacancies in Greater London was double the number of unemployed people, and 15% of bus and 18% of train services had to be cancelled. Direct recruitment from Jamaica and Barbados brought some relief. By 1971, 23% of the staff in London's railways and Underground and 16% of employees in road passenger transport were born abroad. In Wolverhampton, two-thirds of the bus crews were black or Asian, and in Glasgow, more than half of the city's transport department consisted of Indians and Pakistanis. In some places, however, like Coventry, even Indians who spoke English well could not get jobs as bus conductors. In Bristol in 1963, where the Omnibus Company operated a colour bar, a black student, Paul Stephenson, helped to organise a large demonstration, and the buses were successfully boycotted for several weeks before the company finally gave in.

In 1991, 12% of Black Caribbeans, 13% of Pakistanis, 10% of Black Africans, and 8% of Indians were working in transport and communication (mainly the Post Office) compared with 6% of the working population as a whole. In 1993, 6% of British Rail employees were from ethnic minorities, and 16% of them worked as station and yard staff, compared with 2% who were managers or traindrivers. In 1995, 27% of London Underground's 16,153 employees were from non-white ethnic minorities.

One of the most dramatic changes in Britain's transport services over the last thirty years or so has been the growth in mini-cab firms from which cars can be booked by phone but are not licensed to 'ply for hire'. It is a service we now take completely for granted. Prompted by increasing affluence, inadequacies in public transport, improved radio phone technology and lack of regulation, many people from the new groups of immigrants arriving in the 1970s and 1980s set up cab firms, because capital costs were low. Some have also set up coach hire companies.

At the end of 1994, there were some 59,800 licensed taxis in Great Britain. London's share was 18,300 taxis, and it had 21,600 licensed taxi drivers, up from 11,500 in 1965. The number of taxis in the rest of England and Wales was 32,900, and in Scotland about 8,600. One-third of Greater London's black hackney cabs are still owned and run by Jewish people; the meter is known among drivers as a *Zeiger* or a Jewish piano.

▲

Guarding the line at White City Underground. In 1995, 27% of London Underground employees were from non-white ethnic minorities.

▶

In 1958, when this driver and conductor were photographed, there were about 8,000 ethnic minority public transport workers in Britain.

▲

Top: A Bradford bus conductor.

Bottom: More than one in ten of all British Airways staff in 1995 were from non-white ethnic minorities.

In addition, there are some 56,400 licensed private hire cars (including mini cabs) in England and Wales outside London, and about 6,000 in Scotland. In London, where private hire cars do not require a licence, it has been estimated that there are at least 40,000. In the absence of ethnic records, it is not possible to say how many private hire cars are owned and run by people from ethnic minorities. However, informal estimates suggest that the proportion is substantial, particularly in metropolitan areas.

Eight out of ten British Airways' employees work at Heathrow or Gatwick airports, which deal with most of the passengers and cargo moving in and out of Britain. In 1995, more than one in ten of all British Airways staff were from non-white ethnic minorities; only one in fifty were managers. That did not include staff in catering and cleaning, as most of these services have been subcontracted to private companies.

Foreign seamen, or lascars as they were once known, have been used on British ships for hundreds of years because they were cheaper. More recently, ship-owners have sought to avoid higher local wages and conditions by sailing under 'flags of convenience' – such as Panamanian or Liberian – and by hiring foreign seamen. By 1975, 5,800 foreign seamen – one-third of the crew of all deep seafaring vessels – were employed on British ships and paid on average half the wages of a British seaman. This was made possible through an agreement with the National Union of Seamen and a special provision in the 1976 Race Relations Act making it lawful for seamen of different nationalities to be paid differently for the same job. The agreement was cancelled in 1983 and the Act amended accordingly. In 1994, over half the seamen on British ships using the UK as a port, including ferries, were not born in the UK; that is 10,629 out of a total of 20,248 seamen (53%).

MEDICINE AND SCIENCE

t was clear from the outset, when the National Health Service was set up in 1948, that it would be some years before medical schools in Britain produced an adequate supply of qualified doctors and nurses. The success of the NHS depended crucially, therefore, on importing fully trained nursing and medical professionals, as Enoch Powell, Minister for Health from 1961-63, fully recognised.

European Volunteer Workers were first recruited as domestic workers in tuberculosis sanatoria in the autumn of 1946, although many refugees during the war also worked as domestics. They were followed by Italians, under the official Italian scheme introduced in 1950, and later by a steady stream of women from Ireland, Africa, the West Indies, the Indian subcontinent and Malaysia. According to a government report in 1976, 20-25% of hospital domestic staff were black or of Irish origin. Unskilled kitchen staff were drawn mainly from the New Commonwealth countries, while Italians and Spaniards did most of the catering. London teaching hospitals relied most heavily on staff born overseas – in 1969, 37% were born outside the UK.

In 1968, 35% of the 18,708 trainee nurses and midwives born overseas were from the West Indies, 15% were from Ireland, 9% were from Mauritius, and 6% from Malaysia. The rest came from other countries in the New Commonwealth. Most were recruited directly from overseas. By 1975 Malaysia had replaced the West Indies as the main recruitment area for trainee nurses.

Qualified nurses were also continuously imported, mainly to fill the lower grades in social nursing (care of elderly people, people with a mental illness or with learning disabilities). Most of the 4,334 work permits for nursing staff in 1975 went to Malaysians, Caribbeans, Mauritians, Filipinos and West Africans.

In the 1960s, the NHS was still short of between 2,500 and 3,000 doctors and the government made special arrangements to ease the entry of trained doctors into the country when employment vouchers were introduced under the Commonwealth

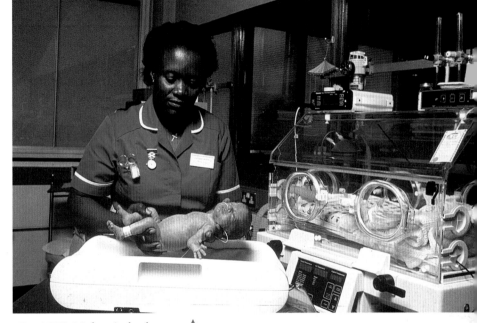

Health in the balance: a midwife weighs a premature baby. In 1968, 35% of trainee nurses and midwives born overseas were from the West Indies.

Behind the scenes: two hospital laundry workers with the day's load.

Sigmund Freud (1856-1939), founder of psychoanalysis, best known for his research on the unconscious mind and his interpretation of dreams, came to London from Vienna as a refugee from Nazi persecution. The house in Hampstead where he spent the last year of his life is now a museum. Portrait by Viktor Kraus.

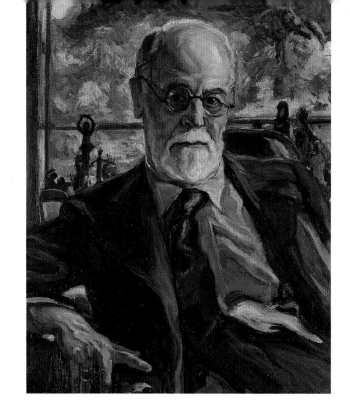

Joseph Rotblat, Emeritus Professor of Physics at the University of London, was born in Warsaw in 1908, and came to Britain in 1939. Together with the Pugwash Conferences on Science and World Affairs, of which he has been President since 1988, he was awarded the Nobel Peace Prize in 1985.

Sir Magdi Yacoub, born in Cairo in 1935, pioneer of heart and lung transplants in Britain.

Abdus Salam FRS, of Imperial College, London, originally from Pakistan, shared the Nobel Prize for Physics in 1979 equally with Stephen Weinberg and Sheldon Glashow of Harvard University. He was also awarded the prestigious Hughes, Copley and Royal Medals.

DOCTORS AND SCIENTISTS

MUHAMMAD AKHTAR FRS, of Pakistani origin, Professor of Biochemistry at Southampton University

J E BANATVALA, of Indian origin, Professor of Clinical Virology at St Thomas's Hospital, London

VIJAY VIR KAKKAR FRCS, of Indian origin, Professor of Surgical Science at King's College School of Medicine and Dentistry and National Heart and Lung Institute, and director of Thrombosis Research at King's College, London

HANS WALTER KOSTERLITZ FRS, of German origin, Emeritus Professor of Pharmacology and Director of Research on Addictive Drugs at Aberdeen University

NAGEENA MALIK, of Pakistani origin, Open University Oxford Research Unit

CESAR MILSTEIN FRS, originally from Argentina, won the 1984 Nobel prize for his work on the immune system. He was also awarded the Wellcome, Royal and Copley Medals

SALVADOR MONCADA FRS, originallly from El Salvador, Director of Research at Wellcome Foundation Ltd

SIR RUDOLPH PEIERLS FRS CBE, of German origin, was appointed Wykeham Professor of Physics at Oxford. Awarded the Royal and Copley Medals

GUIDO PONTECORVO FRS, originally from Italy, Professor of Genetics at Glasgow University until his retirement

HERBERT SEWELL FRCP, originally from Brazil, Professor of immunology, Nottingham University

AZIM SURANI FRS, geneticist at the AFRC Institute of Animal Physiology and Genetics Research at Cambridge

JAMSHED RUSTOM TATA FRS, originally from India, Head of the Laboratory of Developmental Biochemistry at the National Institute of Medical Research, London

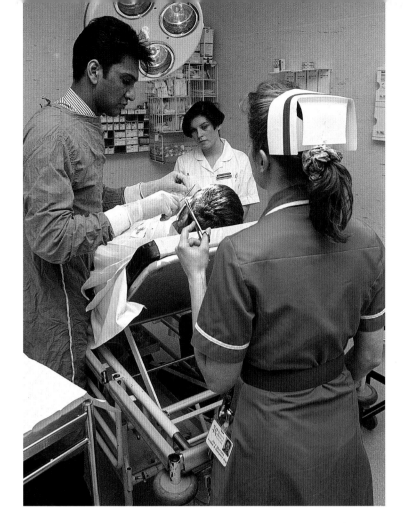

▲

In 1976, over a third of hospital medical staff were born overseas, and about half of the overseas doctors came from the Indian subcontinent. In 1992/3, 23% of doctors in Britain were born overseas.

Immigrants Act in 1962. The shortages were particularly acute in metropolitan areas and in unpopular specialities such as geriatrics, mental health, traumatic and ortho-paedic surgery, and ophthalmology. In 1975, 84% of junior medical hospital staff in geriatrics were born overseas. Essential support services such as anaesthetics and radi-ology also relied heavily on imported labour. In 1976, the Government reported that:

> Though immigrants, including workers from the Irish Republic, account for only about 6% of those economically active in Great Britain ... [in] the National Health Service in England and Wales... over a third of hospital medical staff, about 18% of doctors in general practice, and a little over a fifth of all student and pupil nurses and pupil mid-wives were born overseas.

It was calculated at the time that each doctor recruited overseas saved Britain £28,000 in training. Quite simply, the NHS would never have been able to meet Britain's grow-ing health needs without them.

Around half of the overseas doctors and general practitioners came from the Indian subcontinent and a quarter from the Old Commonwealth and South Africa. A growing number also came from the Middle East, especially after 1970. Some rose to the top of their profession and brought people from all over the world to Britain for treatment. Sir Magdi Yacoub, a cardio-thoracic surgeon, originally from Egypt, pio-neered heart and heart and lung transplants in Britain. Dr A Karim Admani, originally from India, was awarded an OBE in 1986 for his services in the treatment of cere-brovascular diseases. He set up Britain's first stroke unit in Sheffield in 1975.

Besides this front-line contribution to the health of the nation, there are large numbers of immigrant and ethnic minority staff working behind the scenes as x-ray assistants, laboratory technicians, hospital pharmacists, physiotherapists, hospital porters, caterers and cleaners.

In 1993, ethnic minority nurses made up about 8% of the NHS's nursing staff in

An Asian laboratory technician working at the Blood Transfusion Centre. Vital medical research also goes on in the laboratories of teaching hospitals.

A radiographer settles a patient in for an x-ray.

essential areas of social nursing. A recent report suggests that it takes ethnic minority staff five years longer than their white colleagues to reach the higher nursing grades.

With a significant proportion of British-born nurses leaving to work abroad, either permanently or on short contracts, Britain still depends substantially on 'working holidaymakers' from Commonwealth countries such as Australia, New Zealand, Hong Kong, South Africa and Nigeria to make up the shortages. Some hospitals prefer to recruit directly from overseas, especially to fill the least popular jobs. In 1989, for example, the press reported that a Surrey hospital was advertising in the West Indian press (especially in Trinidad) for nursing staff to work in a geriatric hospital.

Preliminary analysis of the 1992/3 Labour Force Survey shows that 23% of all doctors in Britain, 15% of pharmacists, 10% of nurses and 13% of physiotherapists were born abroad.

Invisible to the public is the vital medical research that goes on in the laboratories of teaching hospitals – we experience the results of this work in new medical technologies and cures. For example, Professor Herbert Sewell, from Brazil, a leading authority on immunology at Nottingham University, spent five years with his team developing a vaccine – known as 105AD7 – to treat bowel cancer. The discovery by Dr Nageena Malik of the Open University Research Unit in Oxford that aspirin keeps corneal cells elastic could be used to stop eyes ageing prematurely.

Chinese medical techniques have led the way in the 1980s and 1990s in making alternative health treatments more popular and more widely available in Britain. More people are turning to acupuncture and herbal remedies everyday. Chinese doctors such as D F Luo and Susanna Jiang, who practise in London, are among the growing number who run herbal and acupuncture clinics.

The contributions of immigrant communities to the field of medicine go back to the days when the Huguenots set up a French hospital, which moved to Rochester, Kent, in 1960. In 1884, a successful Italian businessman, Mr Ortelli, established the Italian Hospital, but it unfortunately had to close down in 1989 due to lack of funds.

Medicine and law were the principal subjects that students from the former Empire came to Britain to study. Many stayed on to set up their own practices. As doctors, they were keenly aware of the social changes needed to improve health, and some became actively involved in local politics. Dr Harold Moody, who came to London from Jamaica in 1904 to study medicine at King's College, started his own practice in Peckham in 1913 after being rejected for the post of medical officer to the Camberwell Board of Guardians – 'the poor people would not have "a nigger to attend them",' it was said. He was the founder of the League of Coloured Peoples. Chunilal Katial, who set up the Finsbury Health Centre in Pine Street – an enterprising example of integrated medicine in the days before the NHS – also became the first Asian mayor in Britain in 1938. Dr Jayanti Saggar, who graduated from St Andrews, became Scotland's first Asian councillor in Dundee in 1936. David Pitt, a Grenadan, studied medicine at Edinburgh, and returned to Britain in 1947 from Trinidad where he had worked as a doctor. He practised in Hampstead and went on to become president of the British Medical Association in 1985. He was made a peer in 1975, nineteen years before he died.

There were many others. The Trinidadian, Dr John Alcindor, had a practice in Paddington, and worked for the Red Cross when he was rejected by the army during the war. Dr Alcindor also played an important part in the second Pan-African Congress. Dr Ernest Goffe, a Jamaican, was a doctor at St Ann's General Hospital in Tottenham, London, where he treated the wounded in the First World War. Dr Goffe was a member of the Fabian Society. His son, also a doctor, was a member of the team which developed the polio vaccine. In the nineteenth century, James Jackson Brown from Jamaica ran a practice in Hackney and is remembered for his efforts on behalf of bomb victims. Frances Batty Shand, daughter of a Scottish landowner and a free black woman, founded the Association for Improving the Social and Working Conditions for the Blind in Cardiff, where a plaque was unveiled in 1926 forty years after her death. In 1879-81, a physician at Guy's Hospital, Frederic Akbar Mahomed, son of Sake Deen Mahomed, discovered from his attempts to measure blood pressure clinically that kidney damage was not the cause of hypertension, as widely believed at the time, and that even healthy people could suffer from it.

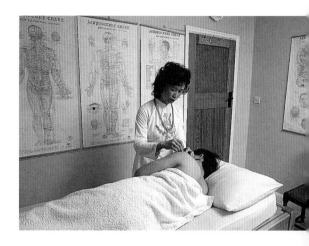

A Vietnamese acupuncturist in Cambridge.

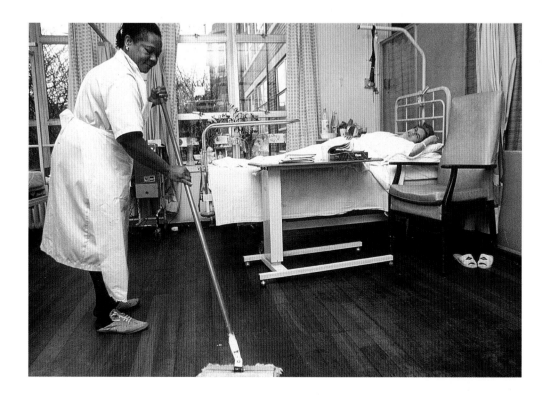

One of the many unsung,
often unseen, workers who help to keep
Britain's health service going.

HOTELS AND RESTAURANTS

fter the Second World War, when cars (and holidays) became more affordable, there was a boom in the hotel and restaurant industry. Charles Forte, whose Italian parents ran a cafe in Scotland, was one of many who made their fortunes at that time. He began with a milk bar in Regent Street in 1935, and only got into the hotel and property business after the war, during which he was interned as an 'enemy alien'.

The demand for hotel and restaurant staff became urgent, and the Hotels and Restaurants Association mounted recruitment drives in the West Indies. Employers also used the work permit scheme to find the workers they needed. In the 1950s, it was Portuguese and Italians; in the 1960s, Spaniards, Filipinos, Turks, Greek Cypriots, Egyptians, Colombians, Moroccans and Poles. The reason employers found it difficult to fill vacancies locally was that the jobs of waiters and waitresses, cooks, chefs, porters, chambermaids and cleaners were among the worst paid, and offered very poor terms and conditions. They involved split shifts, weekend work, and were often part-time. Holidays were few and staff were more likely to be laid off instead.

A Department of Employment study of 43 employers in 1971 made it clear that 33 of the employers had been unable to find staff locally – 12 said that it was because of the pay, 17 that the problem was the shiftwork, and 12 blamed poor working conditions. In 1971, when the total foreign-born population of Britain was 3%, 14% of all hotel workers and 25% of restaurant workers were born abroad. In London, just under half of hotel workers were born abroad.

The hotel and restaurant industries continued to grow as cheaper air travel led to mass tourism. Ethnic minority entrepreneurs were among those who took advantage of the market in order to set up new businesses or diversify into the sector. Gulshan Jaffer's Four Crowns Hotel and Jasminder Singh's Edwardian Group are among the most prominent hotels today.

In 1994, tourism accounted for just under one-third of Britain's service exports. Tourists spent £6 out of every £10 on accommodation and eating out. The industry depends crucially on being able to retain staff in hotels and restaurants. Most tourist-related jobs are in London, followed by the north-west and Scotland, and both hotels and the restaurant trade still rely heavily on immigrants and people from ethnic minorities.

The Radisson Edwardian Hotel at Heathrow won *Business Traveller Magazine's* award for the Best Airport Hotel in the World in 1995. The partnership between Edwardian Hotels and Radisson Hotels Worldwide has created London's largest privately owned hotel group, with ten hotels offering nearly 2,000 bedrooms. The company also has partnerships with 200 London restaurants and pubs, as well as with Centre Stage – a company which brings more than 40,000 tourists to London on theatre breaks.

All smiles: a group of Italian chefs kitted out for work.

In 1994, Chinese food sales amounted to an estimated £366 million – half the value of all 'ethnic' food sales.

In 1981, 27% of black women were likely to be working in cleaning and catering jobs compared with only 11% of women overall. Six years later, an investigation by the Commission for Racial Equality showed that 16% of all hotel employees in Britain were from non-white ethnic minorities, but eight out of ten of them worked in London and Heathrow hotels. Nearly three-quarters worked as cleaners, waiters and porters compared with an overall average of half, and only 2% were in middle management compared with 7% overall. In 1992/3, 24% of all restaurant employees were born abroad, and between 1988 and 1990, 50% of Bangladeshi men, 43% of Chinese men and 33% of Chinese women worked in hotels and restaurants. In 1994, one in ten chefs and cooks, and 15% of all hotel porters, were from ethnic minorities. On 3 March 1996, the *Independent on Sunday* reported that 'there are now 10,000 curry houses in Britain with 60-70,000 employees, and a turnover of £1.5 billion – more than steel, coal and shipbuilding put together'.

The labour and enterprise contributed to the 'hospitality' industry by Britain's ethnic minorities, wherever they were born, is integral to its success. Deducted from the equation, the impact in terms of staff shortages, higher service costs and potentially declining tourist revenue would be quickly felt throughout the economy. If, after 50 years of settlement in Britain, ethnic minorities are still concentrated in unpopular and poorly paid jobs – jobs that are nevertheless vital to the British economy – and still underrepresented in more highly prized areas of work, this only goes to show that the job markets, far from being 'free', reflect continuing racial discrimination and disadvantage.

Setting out the towels at the Tower Thistle Hotel in London.

FOOD AND COOKERY

This teapot and stand, with their Japanese design, were made in the Worcester factory in about 1775, but people in Britain had been savouring a nice cup of tea since the middle of the sixteenth century.

An Italian ice cream seller or 'Hokey Pokey' man, shown in a cartoon by Phil May from the turn of this century.

In 1994, fish and chips had a 14% share of the British food market compared with 18% in 1990. Its popularity was gradually being challenged by 'ethnic' food, the market for which was estimated to be growing at 12% a year. A Gallup poll survey of 1,064 adults in 1995 found that, while a quarter of them visited a fish and chip shop once a month – in Wales and the Midlands almost a third of them did – Chinese food was catching up fast. The detailed picture is shown below.

Total sales of 'ethnic' food in 1994 were valued at about £736 million – Chinese food sales amounted to an estimated £366 million (50%), while Indian food sales came to about £273 million (37%). The most striking fact here is not the competition for market shares – unless one owns a restaurant – but the extraordinary change in British eating habits.

Tea reached Britain from China some time in the middle of the seventeenth century – the first public tea sale was held in 1657. By 1779, 18 million pounds of tea were being consumed every year, about two pounds per person. Fish and chips were probably first sold from a shop in Oldham in 1870.

It is often believed that Indian food was brought here by post-war immigrants from India, Pakistan and Bangladesh. But 'curry' first appeared on an English menu in 1773, at the Norris Street Coffee House in London's Haymarket; and a recipe for fish curry, using curry powder and four or five green apples, appeared in *A Plain Cookery Book for the Working Classes*, published by Charles Elme Francatelli in 1858, with the advice that Patna rice was the cheapest. Francatelli was a leading chef in Victorian times, born in London but of Italian extraction. Clearly, there was a taste for unusual food, even among the poorest people, and basic ingredients were readily available, at least in ports such as London, Cardiff, and Liverpool.

A curry house, Salut-e-Hind, opened in London in 1911, and by the 1930s there were at least two Indian restaurants as we know them today, Shafi's and Veeraswami's. Country inns, too, had curry on the menu. Indian restaurants, however, only became a regular feature of the high street in the 1960s when Bangladeshis began arriving.

The histories of other 'ethnic foods', or initiatives in catering by ethnic minority entrepreneurs, go back to the turn of this century. Isaac Levy came up with the idea of serving food in pubs, mainly for City workers, and Chef and Brewer was set up by his son in 1892. By 1914, the number of J Lyons and Co teashops for 'clerks and lady shoppers' had risen to 200, from one in 1894 – the Trocadero in Piccadilly and the Throgmorton in the City were for better heeled patrons. The first 'Corner House' restaurant was opened in Coventry Street by Joseph Lyons and the Salmon and Gluckstein family in 1907, and offered reasonably priced food. Following an extension

MONTHLY VISITS TO TAKEAWAYS AND RESTAURANTS

	SOUTH	WALES/MIDLANDS	NORTH/SCOTLAND
Fish and Chips	24%	32%	25%
Chinese	20%	22%	19%
Indian	14%	13%	12%

Source: UK Catering Market, Keynote 95.

A Chinese restaurant in London in 1939. After fish and chips, Chinese food is the most popular takeaway or eat out cuisine in Britain.

in 1921, it could seat 4,500 customers. Blooms, in London's East End, opened in 1920 and became famous for its pickled salt beef.

Terroni and Sons was one of the earliest Italian restaurants in London, set up in 1890 in Clerkenwell. There was Gennaro's, the Italian restaurant in Soho, as well as a few fashionable Italian restaurants such as Bertorelli's and Quo Vadis in Soho and Mayfair. Several English restaurants had Italian chefs, and when many of them were interned on the Isle of Man during the war, they cooked for the prisoners. By 1938, the Italians in south Wales had set up 300 cafes, and Italians in Scotland were running some 700 restaurants. In Manchester, Ras Tefari Makonnen, journalist, organiser of the Pan-African Congress and entrepreneur par excellence, set up a chain of teashops where some of the thousands of US black soldiers posted in Britain during the Second World War found an unqualified welcome. In the early years of this century, Chinese restaurants, such as Young Friends, were well-established in the Limehouse area in London, as well as in other ports. Daquise Restaurant, near Brompton Oratory in London, was set up in 1947 by Jan Dakowski, a Polish refugee.

Bloom's in London's East End, one of the most famous of London's cafés, closed in 1996. Morris Bloom started his business in 1920, at 58 Brick Lane, moving to number 2 in 1924. A connoisseur of table delicacies, he developed a new method of pickling salt beef which drew customers from all over the city. He opened another restaurant in Golders Green in 1968.

Expensive restaurants had long imitated French cooking and written their menus in French, while for a good cheap meal, one 'gravitated naturally', as George Orwell put it, towards a Greek, Italian or Chinese restaurant. That was in the 1940s. As for 'English bread', it was all good, he tells us, 'from the enormous Jewish loaves flavoured with caraway seeds to the Russian rye bread which is the colour of black treacle'. In the 1950s, life styles that had previously only been available to the very rich became more widely afford-able. The war and rationing were over and to be forgotten as quickly as possible; there was full employment, and more people had money to spend. In London, the old Chinatown in Pennyfields had been destroyed by bombs, and a new centre was set up in the heart of the West End. Entrepreneurs like Charlie Cheung began adapting Cantonese food to English palates. Chop Suey houses spread, even to remote rural villages. They were open late, and the food was appetising. Even in the late 1970s, the only restaurant open on a Sunday in Inverness was Chinese.

The Chinese were not the only people to see what was happening. A plate of pasta with chianti and cappuccino at one of the multiplying Italian trattoria became a cheap and appetising alternative to pie and two veg. Greek food, too, became popular in the 1960s – with more people taking cheap package holidays to Greece, the growing taste

A basket of ingredients for an Indian meal: Madhur Jaffrey, the celebrated Indian actress, is also a wonderful cook, and has shared her talents through several recipe books and television appearances.

for moussaka, taramosalata and ouzo had to be catered for.

By the 1970s, curry houses had moved from side streets to high streets, and new immigrants from Iran, Lebanon, Cyprus and Turkey were opening their own restaurants and cafes. Kebab stalls jostled beside takeaway curry houses. Traditional English 'chippies', now increasingly run by Chinese, Italian and Greek-Cypriot families, began offering sweet and sour dishes as well as the traditional pies and fried fish. Cypriot, Polish, Iranian, Italian, Chinese and Indian grocers and greengrocers brought in fruit and vegetables that had previously just been names in travel books. Restaurants such as the Hummingbird and the Brixtonian offered Caribbean food. Sandwich bars found room in the new arcades and malls, and did a roaring business, offering more and more exotic (and healthy) fillings. Italian delicatessens and bakeries gave people an alternative to sliced bread and sticky buns. And Jewish bakeries offered bagels with cream cheese.

Now, supermarkets stock a variety of 'instant' curry pastes and powders, every kind of pasta, olive oil, couscous and rice, and, with an increasingly open European market, whole refrigerators full of continental cheeses, cold cuts, sausages and patés. Publishers have got in on the act and new cooking sections have sprung up in bookshops. Not to be outdone, television programmes include experts like Madhur Jaffrey and Anton Mossiman to show anyone who is still diffident about their culinary skills how very easy it really is to move from kippers to kurma. The growing 'ethnic' food manufacturing sector brings out new dishes every day, and whole Italian, Chinese or Indian meals can be bought and warmed up in 20 minutes. On 25 May 1996, *The Financial Times* reported that, according to Sharwood's, a leading 'ethnic' food manufacturer, the market in ethnic food for home cooking – including Indian, Chinese and Thai – is worth £129 million a year in the UK.

Far from being knocked off their stride by such colossal poaching, the restaurant trade is exploring new cuisines and developing more sophisticated marketing techniques. Chinese restauranteurs are switching from Cantonese to Indonesian, Vietnamese, Korean and Thai food, Bangladeshis offer 'baltis' as well as moghlai-style curries, and tapas bars are the latest addition.

It is difficult to imagine returning to the days when going out for a Chinese, Indian or Thai meal would have meant booking a flight instead of a mini-cab.

The Star of India in Old Brompton Road, London.

SPORT

S ome of the most striking, and certainly some of the most public, contributions made by Britain's ethnic minorities have been in the field of sport. Sporting success means more to many people than any number of Nobel Prizes for science or poetry. The ancient Greeks at the height of their civilization took the same view and, in the words of the historian C L R James, believed that:

> ... an athlete who had represented his community at a national competition, and won, had thereby conferred a notable distinction on his city. His victory was a testament to the quality of the citizens. All the magnates of the city welcomed him home in civic procession. They broke down a part of the wall for him to enter: a city which could produce such citizens had no need of walls to defend it.

Given the opportunity, talented sportsmen and sportswomen from Britain's ethnic minorities have reached the top of their game as quickly as anyone else. Often though, they have had to play in unequal conditions; even top players have had to shrug off gibes about their race or colour. The first sport in which they achieved considerable success and a high degree of respect as professionals was boxing, one of the most popular sports of the eighteenth century among all classes.

Bill Richmond, a black pugilist, set up a boxing academy, which included the essayist, William Hazlitt, among its pupils. Richmond recognised the talents of a black pugilist from the USA, Tom Molineaux, and coached him to become a formidable heavyweight fighter. Molineaux's return match against the English heavyweight champion, Tom Cribb, was attended by a record crowd of 15,000, a quarter of them from the local nobility and gentry. James Wharton, the 'half Nubian', came to London in 1820, having learned to fight as a cabin boy on ships sailing to India. He won all of his nine prize fights, and is best remembered for the battle in Staffordshire on 9 February 1836 against Tom Britton of Liverpool. The fight went to 200 rounds and lasted four hours and four minutes. There were as many as 30 well-known Jewish boxers, but the most successful were Daniel Mendoza, a glass cutter's apprentice who set up a boxing school in 1787; and Sam Elias or 'Dutch Sam'. In the twentieth century, Ted 'Kid' Lewis won the British featherweight title in 1913 and the world welterweight crown in 1915. In 1923, Johnny Brown won the British and European bantamweight title – and kept it for five years, and in 1935, Jack 'Kid' Berg claimed the British lightweight title. There were also well-known Irish boxers such as Peter Corcoran, Michael Ryan and 'Sir' Dan Donnelly.

In 1948, the Leamington brothers, Dick and Randolph Turpin, both became British boxing champions. Randolph won the British middleweight title in 1950 and the European and World titles in 1951, defeating Sugar Ray Robinson. John Conteh, from Liverpool, became the world light heavyweight champion in 1974, and has been followed by a succession of black boxers who won world titles, such as Frank Bruno MBE, Lennox Lewis, Nigel Benn and Chris Eubank. 'Prince' Naseem Hamed, born in Sheffield of Yemeni parents, became the world super bantamweight boxing champion in 1994 and the world featherweight champion in 1995; and Billy Schwer is the current Commonwealth lightweight boxing champion. There are of course many others.

▲

Cribb v Molineaux, in front of 15,000. Molineaux lost but he was remembered with admiration:

"A brave man is Molineaux,
*   from America he came*
And boldly tried to enter with Crib
*   the lists of fame ...*
The Black's chance forsook him,
*   he'd not a chance to win;*
He fought like a brave fellow,
*   but was forced to give in, ...*
Tho' beat, he proved a man, my boys,
*   what more could a man do."*

Walter Tull was one of the first black footballers to play for an English professional club, Tottenham Hotspur, in 1909/10. He was dropped the following season after being racially abused during a match at Bristol City. He was killed in action fighting for Britain in the First World War.

▼

The mass popularity of soccer goes back to the last decades of the nineteenth century, and black footballers were present at the outset. Arthur Wharton, Preston North End's goalkeeper, became Britain's first black professional player in 1896. He was also a national sprint champion, and the first athlete to run 100 yards in under 10 seconds at the Amateur Athletics Association Championships in 1886. Walter Tull, the first black outfield player, received enthusiastic press reports when he played for Tottenham Hotspur in 1909/10, although he was dropped after being racially abused at a match in Bristol.

Wharton and Tull were ahead of their time, and it was only in the 1970s that black players began to have a major impact on the game – even though they often had to put up with vicious racial abuse for their efforts. When Cyrille Regis, Brendan Batson and Laurie Cunningham played for West Bromwich Albion, they were dubbed the 'three degrees', and when Remi Moses joined them they became the 'four tops'. In 1978, Nottingham-born Viv Anderson, a full back with Nottingham Forest, became the first black player to be picked for England. Another England international, John Barnes, born in Jamaica, became the first black player to win the Professional Footballers Association's Player of the Year trophy in 1987/88, and the first to be nominated for the Football Writers' Association player of the year. In 1993, Paul Ince became the first black player to captain the England side in a match against the USA. Today, an estimated 25% of professional footballers in England are black.

If there should be any doubt of the 'notable distinction' conferred on the nation by black professional footballers, the transfer sums they fetch today should be sufficient proof of their value. The highest transfer fee ever paid for an English player is

Ian Wright made the leap to professional football relatively late in his life when Crystal Palace pulled him from non-league obscurity in his mid-20s. He won an FA Cup runners-up medal in 1991 before moving to Arsenal where he has consistently been the club's top goal scorer. He has won FA Cup and European Cup Winners Cup honours and been capped 20 times for England.

▼

▶

John Barnes of Liverpool and England was the first black player to receive the PFA's Player of the Year award in 1987/8. He made his name playing for Watford under future England manager Graham Taylor, and came to widespread public attention in 1984 when he scored a stunning individual goal for England against Brazil in the giant Maracaña Stadium in Rio de Janeiro. He has been capped for England 79 times and won two League Championship and two FA Cup winners medals with Liverpool.

£8.5 million, for Stan Collymore when he moved from Nottingham Forest to Liverpool in 1995. That year, too, Andy Cole was transferred from Newcastle United to Manchester United for £7 million, Paul Ince from Manchester United to Inter Milan in Italy for £7 million, and Les Ferdinand from Queen's Park Rangers to Newcastle United for £6 million.

While Irish players have been regulars in the English and Scottish Leagues since their formation, Asians have still to break into the ranks of the professionals. There is one known player of Asian origin at an English club, Chris Dolby at Bradford City, although there have been one or two others in the past. Salim Backi-Khan, from the Mohammedan Sporting Club in Calcutta, played for Glasgow Celtic reserves in 1936/37, while Roy Smith, an Anglo-Pakistani, played for West Ham United in the Football League Division One in 1955/56. Originally from Rawalpindi, he was at the club for five years and played in six first-team games before moving to Cambridge City and then Portsmouth. In the 1970s, Ricky Heppolate played in the first teams of Leyton Orient and Preston North End, while another Anglo-Pakistani, Paul Wilson, was a member of the successful Celtic sides of the Jock Stein era. Shinda Singh had a two-year apprentice contract at Wolverhampton Wanderers and played on the losing side in the FA Youth Cup final in 1976. Franki Su, an Anglo-Chinese professional, played for Millwall, Leicester and Stoke City.

Foreign footballers have also made outstanding contributions to the international reputation of British clubs. Players such as Tony Yeboah from Ghana, Ruud Gullit and Dennis Bergkamp from Holland, Eric Cantona and David Ginola from France, and Claudio Asprilla from Colombia have raised the status and standard of the English Premier League, and its reputation as one of the best in the world. Others like Brian Landrup of Glasgow Rangers, have done the same for Scotland.

Many of England's top county cricket sides have long benefited from foreign players, among them some of the world's best cricketers. Viv Richards, from Antigua, then captain of the West Indies, played for Somerset in the 1970s and 1980s, while Imran Khan, Pakistan's former captain, played for Sussex. Brian Lara, the West Indies' record-breaking batsman from Trinidad, made the highest ever first-class innings score of 501 while playing for Warwickshire in an English county championship match in 1994.

The history of ethnic minority contributions to English cricket is a long one, partly because it was the sport most closely associated with the British Empire, and was exported to the Indian subcontinent and the British colonies in the West Indies and Africa. As C L R James shows in his book, *Beyond a Boundary*, cricket was always more than a game; it was an exercise in character building – expressions such as 'it's not cricket', and 'playing a straight bat' became 'signposts of moral conduct' and the British sense of fair play. Before independence, which was won in the 1940s in the countries of the Indian subcontinent and in the 1960s in the West Indies, British subjects could play for England. And many did.

The most memorable was Prince Kumar Shri Ranjitsinhji, who captained Sussex for 19 years and represented England against Australia in four Test Match series between 1896 and 1902. During a Test against Australia in 1899, placards all over

A princely pose. "He did the impossible and made it commonplace," said one admirer of Prince Kumar Shri Ranjitsinhji. Ranji, as he was known, played for England in four Test Match series against Australia at the turn of the century, and became famous for the deftness of his leg glance. His *Jubilee Book of Cricket* was a bible for children throughout the Empire.

A mixed group: the gentleman players of Essex County Cricket Club in the 1920s.

The Trinidadian, Learie Constantine spent nine years with the Nelson team in the Lancashire cricket league in the 1930s. As well as playing for the West Indies, he was an active campaigner for racial equality in Britain. In 1948, he successfully took the Imperial Hotel to court for refusing him admission 'because he was a nigger', and was awarded £5 token damages. He was knighted in 1962 and created a life peer in 1969, two years before he died.

Ready and waiting: Mark Ramprakash,
a Caribbean-Asian, played first class
cricket for Middlesex in the 1980s and
and has been in the reckoning for the
England Test side throughout the 1990s.

The two Jeremies: Jeremy Isaacs, Director of
the Royal Opera House, with England
rugby union star, Jeremy Guscott.

In a league of his own: Ellery Hanley in
action for Wigan against St Helens in 1989.
Hanley has both played for and coached the
Great Britain rugby league side.

England proclaimed 'Ranji Saves England'. His nephew, Kumar Shri Duleepsinhji, also played from 1924 to 1932, was Sussex captain between 1931 and 1932, and a member of the England side in 12 Tests. Raman Subba Rao CBE played for Surrey and Northamptonshire, and was included in 13 England Test sides between 1951 and 1961; and the Trinidadian, Sir Learie Constantine, was the hero of the Lancashire League in the 1930s.

Basil D'Oliveira OBE, from Cape Town, one of the great names of cricket since the Second World War, played for Worcestershire and England between 1961 and 1980. In 1968, he was selected to play for England in South Africa, but the tour was cancelled when he was refused entry because of his race. Roland Butcher became England's first black Test player in 1981, and others have followed – Philip De Freitas from Dominica, Gladstone Small from Barbados, Chris Lewis from Guyana, Phil Edmonds and Graeme Hick from Zimbabwe, and Devon Malcolm from Jamaica. Malcolm took nine wickets for 57 runs against South Africa at the Oval in 1994, the sixth best bowling figures for any England bowler in a Test Match. British-born Caribbean Asian, Mark Ramprakash, and Nasser Hussain from India, are both Test players, and regularly in the reckoning for the England Test side.

Rugby union, another sport associated with English public schools and exported to the former colonies, has been taken up with international recognition by men such as Jeremy Guscott, Victor Ubogu, Billy Boston, Steve Ojomah and Chris Oti for England. All played for England during the 1990s, its most successful spell ever. Nigel

Streets ahead: Harold Abrahams winning a
220 yard sprint against rivals from Yale and
Harvard universities in 1923. The following
year he won the Olympic 100 metre gold
medal in Paris, a feat immortalised in the
1980s film, *Chariots of Fire*.

Walker played for Wales in the same era. In rugby league, players like Martin Offiah and Ellery Hanley have led the sport into a new, more commercial era. Both are Great Britain internationals, while Hanley also coached the Great Britain team from August 1994 to May 1995, a period that covered a test series against Australia. In 1988, Hanley was transfer-listed for a world record fee of £225,000 after a dispute with his club coach (which was subsequently resolved). In 1995, Ikram Butt became the first Asian to play for England.

In track and field athletics, Jamaican-born Linford Christie has been captain of the British men's team for a number of years. His success is unprecedented – he has won Olympic, World, European and Commonwealth 100 metre titles – and is the only British athlete ever to hold all at the same time. Daley Thompson performed equally startling feats and became a double Olympic, World and European decathlon champion, setting new world records in the 1980s. Other successes include Tessa Sanderson MBE, from Jamaica, who was the Olympic javelin champion in 1984; Fatima Whitbread, of Cypriot origin, who set a world record in 1986 and won a javelin gold medal at the world championships in 1987; Colin Jackson MBE, who was world 110 metres hurdles champion and world record-breaker in 1993; and Kelly Holmes who was the world 1500 metre silver medalist in 1995 and Commonwealth champion in 1994.

The first person from Britain's ethnic minorities, and the first British Jew, to win the British Olympic athletics championship was Harold Abrahams CBE, who took the 100 metre title in 1924. He became President of the Amateur Athletic Association (AAA) and chairman of the British Amateur Athletics Board. Abrahams' achievements were celebrated in the film, *Chariots of Fire*. The first black British athlete to excel internationally was an ex-RAF man, McDonald Bailey, who won a bronze medal in the 1952 Olympic Games, and achieved an all-time record by winning 14 AAA titles for the 100 and 200 yards between 1946 and 1953. Gowry Retchikan is so far the only British athlete of Asian origin to have competed at world level. Of Sri Lankan origin, she was a semi-finalist in the 400 metre hurdles at the 1992 Olympic Games and in the 1993 world championships.

In netball, three of England's latest world championships squad – Cynthia Duncan, Maggie Farrel and Helen Manufor – were from ethnic minorities. No-one succeeded in challenging Walsall-based Desmond Douglas MBE as number one in table tennis in the 1970s and 1980s. Holder of ten English Table Tennis Association titles, he was also the Commonwealth champion in 1985. Daniel Topolski, son of the Polish artist, Feliks Topolski, was a world silver medalist in rowing, and is a very successful coach. Paul Radmilovic, of Irish and Yugoslav origin, won Olympic

Linford Christie's achievements on the track
put him strides ahead of almost every other
British sports star, of this era or any other.
Famous for his power and determination,
Christie has been at the very top of world
sprinting for ten years.

Fatima Whitbread celebrates her
victory at the 1987 World
Championships in Rome.

Undisputed number one:
Desmond Douglas was the top
Briton in table tennis for much of
the 1970s and 1980s.

gold medals for Britain's water polo team in 1908, 1912 and 1920, as well as in swimming in 1905. Flat racing has been dominated by legendary Irish jockeys such as Steve Donoghue, with his six Derby wins in the 1920s and 1930s, Pat Eddery and, most recently, Walter Swinburn. Between 1968 and 1986, Keinosuke Enoeda from Japan built up the Karate Union of Great Britain to 30,000 members and 450 clubs. The Martial Arts Association said that in 1986 there was a 36% increase in the number of participants in martial arts sports, many of them black.

It would not be unreasonable to expect that such accomplishments on the field, in the ring and around the track would qualify dozens, if not hundreds, of ethnic minority sporting figures for management jobs in their particular sport. However, it was not until 1993 that Viv Anderson became professional football's first black first-team manager at Barnsley. He has since moved to become assistant manager at Premier League side, Middlesborough, and his achievement has been followed by Chris Kamara, now manager at Bradford City, and Luther Blissett at Watford. In May 1996, Ruud Gullit became the first black player to take charge of a premier league side when he was appointed first-team coach at Chelsea. Brendan Batson, deputy chief executive of the PFA, has the most senior administrative role of any black person in English football. However, the British Athletic Federation has no-one from Britain's ethnic minorities on its management board nor its council. Nor does the British Olympic Association.

However much ground remains to be covered, ethnic minority sportsmen and sportswomen are an integral part of Britain's sporting life, and the life of the nation.

MUSIC

Ray Man's music shop in London's Covent Garden sells musical instruments from all over the world.

lack musicians have been entertaining British audiences since the early sixteenth century. Elizabeth I had seven black musicians and three black dancers. Cato, Sir Robert Walpole's slave, who was said to 'blow the best French Horn and Trumpet' in eighteenth century England, was passed on as a gift to the Prince and Princess of Wales in 1738.

The following winter was cold, and the musical 'season' froze along with the Thames. The weather was more successful at keeping Italian singers like Signora Cuzzoni away from London than the admonitions of the Irish writer, Jonathan Swift, who had sternly condemned

> ... that Un-natural Taste for Italian music among us, which is wholly unsuited to our northern Climate, and the Genius of our People, whereby we are overrun with Italian Effeminacy and Italian Nonsense.

For nearly half a century Italy had been the source of inspiration for the arts in Britain. George Frederick Handel, who settled in London in 1714, initially wrote Italian operas, and was one of the butts of the cultural chauvinism that seasoned English musical taste. He switched to the oratorio, and became immensely popular among London's Jewish community with compositions such as *Judas Maccabeus*, *Susanna* and *Solomon*. By 1741, opera had finally died out, and only returned in force in 1847 when an Italian, Giuseppe Persiani, bought the lease of the Opera House, had it repaired and opened it as the Royal Opera House.

Black drummers came to Britain with English regiments serving in the West Indies. By 1755, for example, all the drummers in the 4th Dragoons were black. By the end of the century, 'Turkish' music, usually played by black musicians on percussion instruments – cymbals, triangles, tambourines and the 'jingling johnny' – had reached Britain. It inspired both popular and classical music, and certainly George Polgreen Bridgetower would have known it. An exceptional Polish Barbadian

The Fisk University Jubilee Singers were among the most popular black minstrels who visited from the USA. They won the hearts of thousands, including Queen Victoria – who listened with 'manifest pleasure' – with old favourites such as. *Swing Low Sweet Chariot*, *Nobody Knows the Trouble I Seen* and *Roll Jordan Roll.*

musician, he played first violin in the Prince of Wales's private orchestra for 14 years, and performed in 50 public concerts between 1789 and 1799. Beethoven was one of his friends, and would have dedicated his Kreutzer Sonata to him, had the two not fallen out. At that time, black dance music was all the rage in London – 12d secured admission to what were known as 'black hops'. On the streets, the buskers Johnson and Waters were drawing large crowds, not by playing 'African' music, but by dressing up familiar English songs in new rhythms and colours.

In the nineteenth century, the black population of Britain was tiny, and the only opportunity British audiences had to satisfy the taste they had acquired for 'black music' was through visiting minstrels from America. There was William Henry Lane, the dancer, popularly known as 'Master Juba', who fused the Irish jig with Afro-American routines; and James and George Bohee, whose banjo playing had 'every barrel organ play[ing] their favourite banjo song and dance, *I'll Meet Her When The Sun*

The composer, Samuel Coleridge Taylor dedicated his life to integrating black with classical music. People whistled his tunes in the streets, and his pieces were included in concert programmes throughout the country. Following his sudden death from pneumonia in 1912, aged 37, crowds lined the route of his funeral.

Kaikhosru Shapurji Sorabji, son of a Parsi engineer from India and a Sicilian-Spanish soprano, was a prodigious composer, pianist and critic. His prolific output as a composer between 1915 and 1984 included over 100 works, but they were of such length and difficulty that he banned all public performances of them after 1936. *Opus Clavicembalisticum* is four and a half hours long, and his *Organ Symphony No 2* runs to a staggering 396 A3 landscape pages. Sorabji's literary work includes two books of essays and hundreds of articles, reviews and letters. Some of his music has been performed and recorded, and is available through the Sorabji Archive, established in 1988, the year he died, to make his work more widely known.

Goes Down.' In 1864, a law was passed to curb busking after *Punch* magazine launched a crusade against Italian organ grinders who had arrived in Britain after the Napoleonic Wars, but it had little effect. By the 1890s, sheet music for banjo pieces, jigs and cakewalks was selling in millions.

The most popular of all the visitors from across the Atlantic were probably the Fisk Jubilee Singers, who toured England between 1873 and 1877 and delighted audiences everywhere with their spirituals. One review described their music as an 'odd mixture of German part-song, Scottish national airs and Dutch traits'. Black religious music was one of the inspirations for jazz, which in turn was the seed from which popular music grew.

Equally popular during the last two decades of the nineteenth century was the composer, Samuel Coleridge Taylor, son of a doctor from Sierra Leone and an English mother. His life was dedicated to integrating black traditional music with classical music, and his compositions attest to this: *Hiawatha's Wedding Feast, An African Suite, Symphonic Variations on an African Air*, among many others. His music sold in thousands of copies, and he was rated more highly by some of his contemporaries than Sir Edward Elgar. Taylor was also active in the Pan-African movement and contributed to the first issue of Duse Mohamed Ali's *African Times and Orient Review*. From 1903 to his death in 1912 he was professor of composition at Trinity College of Music in London, and conductor of various choral societies. Gustav Holst, the composer of *The Planets*, who was born in Cheltenham of Latvian parents, was 19 years old when Taylor died, and must have known his music.

It was perhaps as well that Taylor did not live to see the days when black British musicians appear to have been expected to play 'ethnic music' only. In the 1950s, the classically trained Trinidadian pianist, Winifred Atwell, made her name by playing a pastiche of ragtime songs. Rudolf Dunbar, a clarinettist, made his conducting debut with the London Philharmonic to a full house at the Royal Albert Hall in 1942, but appears to have faded away from the classical scene; after that he joined Snake Hips Johnson in the dance music world and set up his own band. In 1976, Pearl Connor and some other black musicians effectively challenged the barriers between classical and popular – and white and black – by improvising a jazz version of Bach's *St Lukes Passion* called *The Dark Disciples,* which was broadcast by the BBC.

Some of the greatest classical performers of our time have shared Taylor's belief that music transcends all boundaries. Following his East-West rapprochement with Nehru, independent India's first prime minister, the Jewish violinist, Sir Yehudi Menuhin, and the Indian sitarist, Ravi Shankar, produced the historic performances which served to extend both the western classical repertoire and popular music. Menuhin was president of the International Music Council of UNESCO from 1969 to 1975. He was knighted in 1985 and awarded the Order of Merit in 1987. Another great Jewish musician, the US harmonica player, Larry Adler, built similar bridges between the worlds of 'serious' and 'popular' music. A refugee to Britain from the

McCarthy era, his ease with both Ravel's *Bolero* and Gershwin's *Rhapsody in Blue*, inspired the English classical composer, Ralph Vaughan Williams, to write for him. John Williams, the guitarist, came to Britain from Australia in 1952 at the age of eleven, and has done a lot to popularise the classical repertoire for that instrument. He was awarded the OBE in 1980. In 1995, Bertolt Goldschmidt, a German-Jewish composer, was rediscovered, and his music performed at the 1996 Promenade concerts in London.

The damage done by the musical stereotyping of the 1950s is slowly being repaired. Among the growing number of black and Asian classical performers are Skaila Kanga, a Parsi, who is one of Britain's leading harpists; Gordon Laing, a black contra bassoonist who plays both at the Royal Opera House and as a freelancer; Ian Hall, an organist from Guyana, who has conducted his music in Westminster Abbey; and Willard White, the great Jamaican baritone, who sang the part of Porgy in *Porgy and Bess* at Glyndebourne in 1986, and Wotan in *Die Walküre* in 1989 with the Scottish Opera, as well as acting in *Othello* that year. The Shiva Nova Ensemble, under Priti Paintl, uses sitars, cellos and jazz marimbas; and Wasfi Kani, of Indian descent, is the founder and director of Pimlico Opera. In 1990, within three years of its opening, she launched a programme to take opera into prisons, and is now planning Britain's only eighteenth century, 400-seat lyric theatre.

▲

Larry Adler, the Jewish harmonica player, came to Britain as a refugee from the McCarthy era in the USA. He was equally at ease with 'popular' and 'serious' music. Here he is playing in a Hollywood film of the 1940s, *The Birds and the Bees*. He later wrote the score for the British film, *Genevieve*.

◄

Willard White singing in the Welsh National Opera's 1995 production of *Nabucco*.

Wasfi Kani, founder and director of Pimlico Opera.

▼

Sir Yehudi Menuhin OM, the virtuoso Jewish violinist, has used his music to strengthen international understanding and cooperation. During the Second World War he gave 500 concerts for the Red Cross, and played for survivors of the Belsen concentration camp in 1945.

Hungarian-born Sir Georg Solti made his conducting debut in Budapest in 1938, but left his home country when anti-Semitic restrictions made work impossible. He became a British citizen in 1972 and was knighted in the same year.

Mitsuko Uchida, the Japanese pianist best known for her interpretations of Mozart, is one of the many great musicians who have made their homes in Britain. They include Alfred Brendel, the Austrian pianist; Fou T'Song, the Chinese pianist; Gervase de Peyer, the Swiss clarinettist; Mstislav Rostropovich, the Russian cellist; Bernard Haitinck, the Dutch conductor; and, most recently, Yevgeny Kissin, the young Russian piano prodigy.

Between 1935 and 1955, there was a ban on work permits for US musicians – Duke Ellington was among the last to visit in 1933. It only served to intensify the passionate enthusiasm among white audiences for jazz, irrespective of colour, culture or nationality. Joe Harriott, Britain's legendary alto saxophonist, sailed here from Jamaica in 1951, and immediately set his own musical agenda. Over the years he scored music for the London Philharmonic, and provided the jazz for John Mayer's double quintette, made up of five Indian musicians playing tabla, sitar, and other instruments, with Mayer on the harpsichord and violin – the group was called Indo-Jazz Fusions. The inscription on Harriott's grave stone reads, 'Parker there's them over here can play a few aces too.' Andy Hamilton, the Birmingham tenor saxophone player; Julian Joseph, on the piano; Shake Keane on the flugelhorn and trumpet; and Gail Thompson on the tenor saxophone have all contributed at different times to a vital British jazz scene. Thompson, who set up a successful women's jazz group called

▲

Celebrating his 72nd birthday at a
Birmingham pub in 1990, tenor
saxophonist Andy Hamilton, jamming
with his son Graeme (trumpet), a member
of the 'Fine Young Cannibals', former
'Jazz Messenger', Jean Toussaint (tenor
sax), and Steve Ajao (alto sax).

Gail Force, was co-founder of the Jazz Warriors with Courtney Pine, the tenor saxophonist whose album, *To the eyes of creation*, with Dennis Rollins on the trombone, has
been called the 'most integrated work, fusing African, Caribbean, American, and
European music', uniting soul singers, reggae rhythms, and Courtney Pine's two
inspirations: Bob Marley and John Coltrane.

Since the 1950s, the creativity of black musicians in Britain has largely been
directed towards popular music, influenced by musical trends in the USA and the
Caribbean. The first Caribbean music to be heard on the British air waves in the late

1940s was the Trinidadian calypsos
of musicians such as Lord
Kitchener and Lord Beginner,
whose *Victory Test Match* calypso
became hugely successful.

As the black community in
Britain grew, they began importing
LPs from Jamaica, particularly
recordings of early reggae, as well
as making their own records.
British groups such as Steel Pulse
and Aswad only got their break,
though, when the alliance between
punk and reggae groups in the late
1970s Rock against Racism concerts awakened interest among DJs
and the big companies. At the same
time, the search for a new dance
music found British groups recy-
cling, or experimenting with, American soul and Jamaican reggae.
Black groups such as Linx broke
away from American soul to create
a distinctive new dance music.

◄

Courtney Pine, tenor saxophonist, has played
a large part in the surge in popularity of
modern jazz among young British audiences
in the 1980s and 1990s.

. . . but not forgotten. In fact, not even gone – in 1996 she sold out six shows at the Royal Albert Hall in London. Here, a young Bassey advertises her latest recording.

Aswad in action.

In 1988, Loose Ends became the first black British group successfully to export its sound back to the USA, and a year later Soul II Soul's single, *Back to Life*, reached number one in the British charts. Jazzie B, their lead musician, was recognised for his 'contributions to black music' with an award from the National Association for the Advancement of Coloured People in the USA. Soul II Soul's success also helped British groups to loosen their reliance on the pirate stations that had mushroomed in the 1980s, by making record companies and mainstream radio stations more receptive to the potential mass market for black British musicians' work. The Nigerian-born singer and songwriter, Seal, has sold millions of records, including two top ten albums. His world-wide hit, *Killer,* a collaboration with dance artist Adamski, won praise for its unique mix of house and soul music – a combination pioneered by British artists – and for its anti-racist lyrics. Artists such as Carleen Anderson, Omar and Mica Paris, and more recently Eternal, Michelle Gayle and MN8 have also had enormous commercial success.

In the 1990s, artists such as Massive Attack – who have worked with the Pakistani qawwali performer, Nusrat Fateh Ali Khan – and Tricky have mixed dub with hip hop. jungle, or drum 'n' bass, a fusion of diverse musical styles that grew out of the raves of the early 1990s, introduced breakbeats from hip hop into house and techno music.

Seal, the Nigerian-born singer, has sold millions of records of soul and house music around the world.

Below left: Freddie Mercury of Queen, a Parsi by origin, was one of British rock music's most flamboyant performers in the 1970s and 1980s.
Below right: Singer and songwriter Joan Armatrading.

It's a dog's life: Goldie, jungle music's most successful artist yet, his friends, and their hats.

Vocal band, MN8, and, below, Skin, of the 1990s rock/rap band, Skunk Anansie.

With his album, *Timeless,* Goldie has been recognised as one of drum 'n' bass's principal innovators and its first mainstream star.

The 1980s saw the arrival of bhangra, another hybrid, borrowing from Punjabi musical traditions, Hindi film scores, Afro-American hip-hop, Caribbean idioms and the electronic media. Groups such as Alaap, Heera, Apna Sangeet, DCS, Golden Star, the Sahotas, and artists like Gurdas Maan and Malkit Singh became immensely popular, mainly through performances at weddings and Punjabi community events. It has been suggested that bhangra tapes sell well enough to go gold on national charts, but they are distributed mainly through the Asian community. Bhangra is now being fused with other western musical forms such as reggae and hip hop, most successfully by artists such as Apache Indian, who brought 'bhangramuffin' into the mainstream and successfully exported it back to India through the British pop charts. Other groups such as Asian Dub Foundation, The Kaliphz, Fun-Da-Mental, Bally Sagoo and Bedouin Ascent are expanding the genre all the time.

Dance music is not the only pop genre where British ethnic minorities have made significant contributions. Britpop superstars Echobelly enjoy massive chart and critical success with their unique brand of guitar-driven pop. Echobelly's vocalist, Sonja Aurora Madan, is of Asian descent, and her guitarist, Debbie Smith, of Caribbean origin. The black singer, Skin, and her London-based band, Skunk Anansie, have reached the top ten with a mix of heavy metal, rap and blues. Other fusions, cross-overs and syntheses have produced groups such as the Welsh dub/metal band, Dub War, and Martin Okasili's Nigerian and Irish fusions.

Meanwhile Sufi qawwalis, Afro-Cuban salsa and lambada, Welsh harps, Scottish fiddles, Irish folk songs, Northumbrian pipes, Zairean soukous, Ghanaian high life, juju music from Nigeria, traditional Chinese, Bulgarian and Cajun music, and classical forms and instruments from an extraordinary variety of cultures are all being drawn into service. The Brotherhood see

FUNKI DRED

JAZZIE B grew up in Finsbury Park, north London. He is the leader of the ground-breaking group Soul II Soul, known as the 'Funki Dreds', which has had a profound influence on the development of British dance music, and runs a recording studio in north London.

Soul II Soul started out as a sound system in the 1980s, playing at parties, before making their own distinctive London soul music. Their first album, *Club Classics Vol. 1*, appeared in 1989, and from it came the single *Back to Life*, which reached number one in the charts, and *Keep on Movin*.

Soul II Soul have been one of the most successful black British groups in the USA, where they were awarded three Grammies, plus an award from the US black civil rights organisation, NAACP.

"I went to school with people from many different nationalities and religions – from Greeks to Asians, from Asians to Jews, from Jews to Muslims, from Muslims to Catholics, from Catholics to Rastafarians.

"In my later school years I inherited one of my brothers' sound systems. From there I hooked up with my partner, Daddae Harvey, and we went on to build our own sound system. People appreciated the music we were making so much that we came up with the idea of selling records. We successfully secured a record deal [with Virgin Ten] and the rest is self-evident.

"Our music could only have happened in Britain at that particular time, when everyone was naive and susceptible to almost anything that was going on. It was definitely, without doubt, a British thing. Growing up in the 1970s we were exposed to so many different styles. The foundation was reggae, but I listened to everything from Eddy Grant and The Equals to David Bowie and punk. We just moved with whatever was moving us at that time. The fact that we were brought up in Britain, with that mix of cultures, meant we took a little bit of everything and blended it in with our own style.

"Our roots are very important but when we delve back into them, things are more complex. I go back to the Caribbean and they call me English, and yet when I am here in Britain I might be told to go back to my own country. So what is black British?"

▲

Young Asians began listening and dancing to bhangra music in the late 1980s, combining the traditional sounds of Punjabi and Hindi music with hip-hop, reggae and techno rhythms. Here Asians bop to banghra at the Kudos Club in Watford.

themselves as 'a global thing', and Lakshminarayana Shankar improvises on a 10-string violin.

The musical forms that make up the world of popular music in Britain today are not separate entities, but rather the products of ceaseless exchanges – between music makers, their diverse musical inheritances, and their listeners. There is no single entity such as 'Asian music' or 'black music', if that means music made and played only by or for Asian or black people. If there are any enduring characteristics of popular music and culture, they are its pluralism, its liberality of taste, its disrespect for boundaries, its gift for migration across musical styles and forms. Attempts have been made to tag music – and most art forms – with ethnic labels, and sometimes even to stifle it, but they have always been doomed.

British white musicians have been among the most enthusiastic supporters and imitators of some of the musical styles developed by black artists, so much so that in 1983 a white group, New Order from Manchester, went to the top of the 'black music' chart in the US magazine, *Billboard*. Ethnic minority musicians have needed this enthusiasm, as well as support from DJs, radio promoters, record shops and record companies, to take their music to the widest audiences and markets – the British ethnic minority population, unlike that in the USA, is far too small to sustain an exclusive market, even if that were desirable. The only atmosphere in which the work of black musicians in Britain can flourish is one where there is a free exchange of ideas between all groups. Kanya King, organiser of Mobos, the newest black music awards, recognises this when he says 'we've called ourselves the Music of Black Origin to give ourselves the widest possible musical agenda.'

In 1991, 14,800 – or 4% – of the people who worked in one or other branch of 'culture' were from Britain's ethnic minorities, and ethnic minority musicians made up about 4% of all musicians in Britain. Black Caribbeans were the group most likely to be musicians, followed by Other Blacks, which includes people of mixed origin and those who describe themselves as Black British.

In 1993, exports from Britain's music industry totalled £1,158 million, contributing a net trade surplus of £571 million, similar to that of the steel industry. This total includes revenue from recordings, publishing, performances and the sale of instruments, but does not include music that does not appear in the charts, such as Irish, country and western, and bhangra. While it is impossible to separate the contribution each ethnic group has made to the resounding commercial success of the music industry, it is undeniable that the exchange of musical ideas between Britain's diverse ethnic minorities and the rest of the population over the last fifty years has transformed British musical culture beyond recognition.

Models Naomi Campbell and Moose.
▼

FASHION

Musical styles spawn their own subcultures and distinctive looks – zoot suits; wraparound shades; black berets; velvet collars; double-breasted suits; electric blue two-tone suits; red, gold and green hats; dreadlocks and beaded braids; batik; tams; wristbands; 'urban commando chic'; baggy blue jeans; tracksuits and trainers; chunky gold chains; and nose rings – many drawing inspiration from the materials, designs and fashions of Britain's ethnic minority communities and their original countries.

Fashion no longer 'trickles down' from a wealthy coterie who can afford to sport a new look every day, it 'bubbles up' from the streets and clubs, firing the imaginations of advertisers, photographers, and fashion designers such as Joe Caseley-Hayford, Rifat Ozbek, John Galliano and Bruce Oldfield (below left) and hits the catwalks through 'super models' such as Naomi Campbell (here wearing a Rifat Ozbek design). Campbell is one of a long line of successful black British models which goes back to the sixties when Black Boys established itself as a model agency specialising in finding black models for shows and fashion shoots. At the time black models such as Donyale Luna and Naomi Simms were at the height of their careers.

The demand for 'ethnic' models continues today. Atesh, for example, is the son of Turkish-Cypriot parents, while Moose (right), is Asian. He originally planned to go into pharmacy, but was diverted by an advertisement for 'ethnic models' placed by Ziggy at Z Models agency. He has since worked for British designers such as Katherine Hamnett and, although his international career took off when he modelled for French designer, Jean Paul Gaultier, Moose believes that it was London's multi-racial population that opened the door for him – "It wouldn't have happened anywhere else," he says.

DANCE

Anna Pavlova, who was born in Russia in 1881, began her dancing career with the famous Diaghilev Ballet. She became popular when she set up her own company and took ballet to places that had never seen it before. Her reception in Britain, which was her home after 1912, prepared the ground for the establishment of a national ballet. Here she dances the part of Radha in one of the Krishna stories from the *Mahabharata*. The ballet was choreographed by M F Uday and the music composed by Comoleta Bannerji.

▶

Benazir Hussain, Royal Ballet soloist since 1994, as Profane Love in Ashton's *Illuminations*. Born in Madras, Hussein's family moved to England when she was a child, and she became a star pupil at the Royal Ballet School. She dances a wide range of roles, including Queen of the Wilis in *Giselle* and the Lilac Fairy in *Sleeping Beauty*.

ance did not receive formal state recognition or royal patronage in Britain until 1946 when the Arts Council was set up, but its history goes back to the seventeenth century when the masque, a British version of French court ballet, was popular at the English court. London was a centre of ballet during the next two centuries. In the eighteenth century, a number of French dancers came to London and helped to make ballet popular, most significantly Marie Sallé, who performed at Covent Garden as a nine-year-old in 1716, and caused a furore in 1725 when she danced in a Grecian tunic and sandals with her hair down. Handel composed his only ballet especially for her in 1734.

Other important dance figures of the time included Charles Didelot and Jules Perrot from France and the Danish dancer, Dame Adeline Genée, who came to Britain in 1897 and was principal dancer at the Empire Theatre in Leicester Square for ten years; she died in Surrey in 1970.

In the early twentieth century, the most influential dancers were of Russian origin. The most famous of these, Anna Pavlova, who some claim is of Jewish background, came to Britain in 1910. Two years later, she moved in to Ivy House in north London which, since her death in 1931, has been a museum dedicated to her and her work. The Central Reference Library near Leicester Square in central London now houses the Anna Pavlova Memorial Library. The acknowledged father of modern dance theory, Rudolf von Laban, emigrated from Germany to England in 1937. While here, he developed an analysis of the principles of human movement; his name and ideas are preserved by the Laban Centre of Dance, based in London.

Two further major influences on twentieth century dance were Marie Rambert and Frederick Ashton, both immigrants to Britain. Rambert was born in Warsaw in 1888 and moved to London in 1913 where she formed the Ballet Club, which became the Ballet Rambert in 1935. It switched its emphasis to contemporary dance in the

1960s, and changed its name to the Rambert Dance Company in 1987. It is now one of four or five leading dance companies in Britain. Ashton, who was born in Ecuador and grew up in Peru, became a choreographer under Rambert's influence after being sent to school in England. He created at least twenty ballets for Rambert in the 1920s and 1930s before working for the Royal Ballet. In 1948, he choreographed the first full-length British ballet, *Cinderella*, and is widely credited with having defined a British ballet style.

The Royal Ballet itself was originally called the Vic-Wells Ballet, and Ninette de Valois, an

Irish woman whose real name was Edris Stanus, played a major role in establishing it. In the 1930s, Maude Lloyd and Frank Staff from South Africa were important dancers there, as was Robert Helpmann from Australia.

Following his defection from the Soviet Union in 1961, Rudolf Nureyev became a permanent guest artist at the Royal Ballet, at the request of Margot Fonteyn. Nureyev's spectacular style is said to have redefined the acceptable limits of male behaviour on the stage. The American choreographer, Martha Graham, brought her dance company to London at about the same time, and in 1967, the London Contemporary Dance School (now also the London Contemporary Dance Theatre) was established at The Place, near Euston. It was the only school in England authorised to teach the Graham technique. In recent years, the company has included several ethnic minority dancers and choreographers, such as Darshan Singh Bhuller, Kenneth Tharp and Isabel Tamen.

The Place is now also home to the Academy of Indian Dance and the Shobana Jeyasingh Dance Company. Classical Indian dance in Britain is taught by at least 30 professional trainers. They teach both Kathakali, a mimed, highly symbolic ballet, traditional to the Malabar coast of west India, and Bharata Natyam, originally the dance of temple dancers in Tamil Nadu in south India. Nahid Siddiqui, from Pakistan, has her own dance company, and has employed several British Asian professional dancers such as Sonya Kundi and Akram Khan. Indian dance is also extremely popular as a recreational activity among Britain's Asian community, and thousands of young people are taught in 'corner shop' classes.

New companies are springing up all the time. RJC was set up by Edward Lynch, Donald Edwards and Les Hamilton to find 'a new black British choreographic

▲
Young ballet students.

A dancer in the Bi Ma company's *4 Gestures*. Bi Ma was founded in 1991 by dancer and choreographer, Pit Fong Loh, who came from Malaysia in 1987 to study at the London Contemporary Dance School. Her choreography fuses the flowing dance movements of the east and martial arts style acrobatics with Western balletic traditions.

▼

language'. The Phoenix Dance Company in Leeds has similar aims, but a highly distinctive dance technique – black British dance encompasses a rich diversity of styles. Pedro Sandiford, a product of the London Contemporary Dance Theatre who has been working with Diversions Dance Company in Cardiff, believes that dance is moving away from performance and becoming spectacle, with technology opening limitless scope for visual effects. Akram Khan also has his own company through which he explores various combinations of kathak and contemporary western dance. Pit Fong Loh founded the Bi Ma dance company in 1991, and her *4 Gestures* was premiered at *Re: Orient*, a festival of Chinese contemporary dance and theatre at The Place in 1995. She won the Paul Hamlyn Foundation Award for choreography in 1995. Jayachandran's Imlata Dance Company combines Indian dance, martial arts and contemporary western dance in creations such as *jyro-scape*.

Even techniques that appear totally opposed to each other, such as western classical ballet and Bharata Natyam are being reconciled through ceaseless experiment and imagination. 'For a ballet dancer,' says Shobana Jeyasingh, 'pointing her foot is the essence of grace, and flexing it is therefore a comic inversion of the norm.' Dance in Britain today is breaking all the moulds, and the new languages that are being developed belong to a home-grown, but global, culture.

▶
Dawn Donaldson, Stephen Derrick and Martin W Hylton in the Phoenix Dance Company's *Heart of Chaos*, choreographed by Darshan Singh Bhuller. Phoenix is based in Leeds.

SHOBANA JEYASINGH

Since 1988, Shobana Jeyasingh has been artistic director of the Shobana Jeyasingh Dance Company, based at The Place Theatre, London. Her choreography for the company includes *Configurations* (1988), *Making of Maps* (1992), *Romance . . . with footnotes* (1993), and *Raid* (1995). She has also produced work for television, film and theatre. In 1993 she received an Arts Council Women in the Arts Project award, and her company was overall winner of the Prudential Award for the Arts. She was awarded an MBE in 1995.

Born in Madras, India, Shobana's early life was divided between India, Sri Lanka and Malaysia, where she had a 'very English education'. She came to Britain to study English literature at Sussex University and, after completing her Masters degree on Shakespeare, became a dancer. Bharatha Natyam, the classical south Indian dance form, remains the basis of her company's work, although her choreography now draws on many other influences.

Shobana Jeyasingh ...

"I knew so much about Britain when I came here, I took it for granted that people would know about India, Sri Lanka or Malaysia. It took me some time to realise that that was not the case at all. To the bulk of the British people India was still a magical, mystical place; either it was some kind of poor third world beggar nation, or it was full of swaying palm trees.

"I wanted to challenge these images, so I began to dance Bharatha Natyam. Then after staying in Britain for so many years I became part of the migrant culture, and I began to have a different idea of what culture is. The term 'ethnic art' just meant people with brown and black skins doing 'pure', naive, non-abstract, or literal work – the label is a stupid picture of the world and it is condescending. Ultimately, behind it there is a feeling that somehow sophisticated thinking can only belong to white people, that brown people can only do cave paintings. Bharatha Natyam is not naive, it is a very sophisticated art form. My dancing and choreography changed because I wanted it to have something to do with my own life, for it to be personal and contemporary. Now my choreography represents a culture which, I think, is true for everybody who lives in cities all over the world.

... and some of her dance company in performance.

"All urban cultures are migrant. People in towns are all migrants from something – from their past or from their youth – because the essential quality of urban life is that you change, that there are no absolutes. All urban centres are multicultural whether people like it or not. Even very English people are inevitably multicultural and they can't help it – they are multicultural because they have access to a mix of cultures.

"People live very complex lives everyday. Take an Indian woman who lives in Britain – she might jet around the world, she might choose to wear a sari in the evening, she might wear a three-piece suit to go to work, she might be in business talking to Japan one day and the USA the next, she might have an arranged marriage, she might send her children to British public schools – we mix and match and make a very interesting cocktail of whatever we want to have or not have. But when it comes to the arts then people somehow, strangely enough, expect it to be

exactly the opposite. When it comes to art you are not supposed to make this interesting cocktail, you have to be authentic in a terribly limited way. All I am doing in my art is actually making the same choices that most Indians, and others, make in their personal lives.

"I try to reflect the influences on my life. In many ways these are outside my control – but they are vast. I have an immense freedom and access to lots of different kinds of music and movement. These are the resources from which I make dance, whether they change anybody or anything I can't really say."

THEATRE

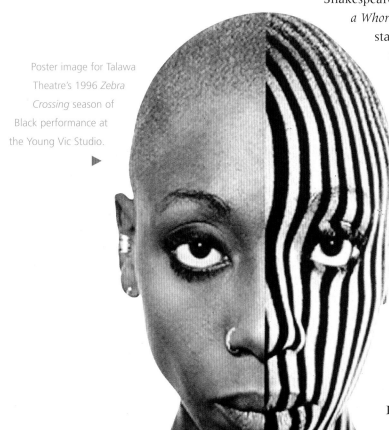

Naseeruddin Shah, in the title role of the Tara Arts/National Theatre co-production of *Cyrano*.

Poster image for Talawa Theatre's 1996 *Zebra Crossing* season of Black performance at the Young Vic Studio.

With mainstream theatre increasingly providing 'safe' entertainment for the tourist market, the most creative work in British theatre today is taking place on the fringe and in regional theatres up and down the country. Unimpeded by the massive commercial demands of the West End, fringe theatre gives free rein to those with the ability and courage to say what has not been said before, in experimental, original ways. Some ethnic minority directors use theatre to dramatise their own experiences as members of minority groups in Britain, while others reinterpret western 'classics' through theatrical forms from other cultures. Their unconventional approach once meant exclusion from London's West End, where commercial criteria determine the fate of every proposal.

But things are slowly beginning to change. Audiences are becoming more sophisticated, partly as a result of the increasingly diverse offering on British television and radio, and mainstream theatre has begun to recognise the considerable commercial pull of exciting fringe productions. Talawa Theatre Company, which was set up ten years ago as a touring company with one show a year produced from Yvonne Brewster's back bedroom, is now one of Europe's leading black theatre companies – Talawa means 'strong'. Tyne Theatre was the first company to co-produce with Talawa – Oscar Wilde's *The Importance of Being Earnest* – and was followed by several others, including the Everyman Theatre, which co-produced *Antony and Cleopatra* with Talawa for the first time ever with a black cast and a black director. In 1993, Yvonne Brewster received an OBE for her services to the arts. These included her direction of Lorca's *Blood Wedding* for the Royal National Theatre and *Romeo and Juliet* for BBC TV, and Talawa's extraordinary range of productions, from Wole Soyinka's *The Road* to Shakespeare's *King Lear* and sell-out performances of John Ford's *Tis Pity she's a Whore* in 1995. Talawa has also extended the repertoire of the British stage, by giving opportunities to new British playwrights, by including international playwrights such as the Cuban, Jose Triana, in their seasons; and by giving young ethnic minority directors the chance to realise their ideas – Indhu Rubasingham recently produced Ibsen's *A Doll's House* as the story of a mixed race relationship.

Kenyan-born Jatinder Verma's theatre company, Tara Arts, which was founded in 1976, has an international reputation for its highly successful adaptations of Indian literature for the stage, and its translations of European literature into an Indian idiom and context. A recent co-production with the National Theatre brought a new version of *Cyrano* to the stage, with Naseeruddin Shah in the title role. The play toured the UK before travelling to six Indian cities.

Theatro Technis, set up by George Eugeniou, among others, will be 40 years old in 1997. From its first production, *A Night without End*, to its most recent one, *Harsh Angel*, Theatro Technis has explored the human tragedy of partition in Cyprus. It has also brought Greek and Spanish theatre to London, most recently Federico Lorca's *Blood Wedding*, and has

▲ ▲ ▶

Since Sheridan's time, in the 18th century, Irish playwrights have made a substantial contribution to British theatre. Sean O'Casey spent much of his working life here, as did Oscar Wilde (above) and George Bernard Shaw (right).

◀

Theatro Technis's *Harsh Angel*, by Maria Avraamidou, a play about the partition of Cyprus.

opened its doors to other groups such as Tara Arts, Clean Break, Temba – a company set up by Alton Kumalo, Norman Beaton, Pearl Connor, and Michael Abensetts – Jean Baptiste Dance Company and the Indian Academy of Dance. Black Theatre Co-operative was formed in 1978 to give opportunities to black actors, writers and directors, and it opened with Mustapha Matura's very successful *Welcome Home Jacko*. Tamasha Theatre was established by Sudha Bhuchar, who played Meena in *Eastenders*.

Irish-born actress Fiona Shaw as Shakespeare's Richard II.

▼

Theatro Technis, Talawa, Tara, the Black Theatre Co-operative, Temba, and Tamasha are just some of the numerous ethnic minority companies on the fringe which have injected a new vibrancy into British theatre by expanding its horizons, and helped to reinforce its reputation as one of the best in the world.

In 1991, 2,300 of the 14,800 ethnic minority 'cultural workers' in Britain described themselves as actors, entertainers, stage managers, producers and directors. Including the 1,100 photographers, camera, sound and video operators, this area accounted for 23% of all ethnic minority cultural workers; it covers television, film and radio as well as theatre. Black Caribbeans and Other Blacks, which includes people of mixed

Ira Aldridge as Aaron in a nineteenth-century production of Shakespeare's *Titus Andronicus*. His performance of Othello in 1830 was greeted with outrage and boycotts, which forced him to leave the West End for Europe, where he met with acclaim.

Hugh Quarshie in Vanburgh's *The Relapse* or *Virtue in Danger*.

origin and those who describe themselves as Black British, were most likely to belong to this group.

The controversy over integrated casting, which in Britain means black actors taking 'white parts', is still revived now and again, for example over the casting of a black actor as Mr Snow in *Carousel*. Adrian Lester's Rosalind in Shakespeare's *As You Like It* attracted more attention because he was playing a female role than because he is black. Joe Dixon, artistic director of the Comédie Anglaise, received the *Sunday Times*'s, Royal National Theatre Ian Charleson Award for his performance as Jacques in Cheek by Jowl's production of *As You Like It*, and recently played Antonio to Juliet Stevenson's Duchess in Webster's *The Duchess of Malfi*.

The days are past when the West End could boycott a black actor for playing Othello, which was what happened to Ira Aldridge, a US actor, in the 1830s. The reviewer for the *Athenaeum* at the time thought it 'impossible that Mr Aldridge should fully comprehend the meaning and force of even the words he utters', and protested 'in the name of propriety and decency' against 'a lady-like girl like Miss Ellen Tree' being 'pawed about on the stage by a black man'. The relentless press campaign against Aldridge left him no choice but to take his talents to the provinces and to Europe, where he was given a rousing reception. When he returned to London as Chevalier Ira Aldridge, Knight of Saxony, he was reluctantly allowed to act at The Lyceum.

Paul Robeson, the US black singer and actor who lived in London for about 12 years after his passport was impounded in 1922 by the US government because of his communist political beliefs, played Othello to Peggy Ashcroft's Desdemona in 1930, and met with some of the same objections as Aldridge. Robeson also collaborated with CLR James to put on a stage version of James's *Black Jacobins* in 1936. Robeson's greatest success, though, was as a singer. His concert at St Paul's Cathedral was packed out, and 5,000 people thronged outside to hear his powerful baritone voice singing *Ol' Man River* through loudspeakers. Robeson went on to become the first black actor to play the leading role in a British film in 1935 – *Sanders of the River*, produced by the Hungarian immigrant, Alexander Korda. It was followed by *Song of Freedom*, *Big Fella*, *King Solomon's Mines*, *Jericho*, and *The Proud Valley*, shot in 1937 in the Rhondda Valley.

In the eighteenth century, British theatre and pantomime were strongly influenced by the talents of immigrants, not only as actors but as set designers and costume artists. British stage sets had been fairly austere until Philippe Jacques de Loutherbourg was hired as a scene painter for Drury Lane by the actor and producer, David Garrick. De Loutherberg introduced more 'realistic' scenery – cloud effects, transparent scenery, and even sketches that had been painted in the South Seas during Captain Cook's final voyage. He also set up an Eidophusikon in Lisle Street in

1781, a 10 foot wide box within which a series of 'moving' or mechanically operated scenes were displayed, an early precursor of the cinema.

Italian drama dominated the English stage as much as the concert hall, and Harlequin, Columbine, Punchinello and all the other figures from Italian comedy were introduced to Britain by Italian artists – Joey Grimaldi, the son of an Italian ballet master, became the greatest British clown. At the end of the nineteenth century, Yiddish theatre provided both Jewish and non-Jewish audiences with some of the most popular entertainment in London – *The King of Lampedusa* was sold out for 200 performances. In 1987, the partnership of Henry Ariel, Bernard Mendelovitch and Anna Tzelnicher, who performed as a travelling troupe, came to an end, and with it Yiddish theatre in London.

The fertile exchange of ideas between the diverse cultures of Britain's most recent ethnic minorities, and the traditions and conventions of British and European theatre, has only just begun, and the new insights and exciting metaphors invigorating the British stage today are proof, if any were needed, that the future is bright.

▲

Joey Grimaldi, who became the 'king of clowns', was born in London in 1779, son of an Italian actor.

◀

The Alexandra Theatre, Stoke Newington, was a drama school and theatre where the best of Yiddish drama could be seen. It closed in 1950.

TELEVISION, FILM AND RADIO

No single medium in history has ever had as much power as television to shape the culture of a nation. What it does not show or say can be almost as eloquent as what we do see and hear. The dramatic change in the way people from ethnic minorities are represented on television can only be fully appreciated by watching current programmes such as *The Real McCoy*, and early sitcoms such as *Love Thy Neighbour* and *Fosters* in quick succession.

Even in the early years of television there were several excellent ethnic minority actors – Carmen Monroe, Pauline Henriques, Errol John, Saeed Jaffrey, Thomas Baptiste and Earl Cameron – but opportunities for them were limited, until well into the 1970s. There were some exceptions: *Passage to India*, directed by Waris Hussein, with Zia Mohyeddin as Dr Aziz, was Play of the Month in 1965; and John Elliot's six-part drama serial, *Rainbow City*, gave the award-winning playwright, Errol John, a leading part as a Jamaican lawyer in a racially mixed marriage in Birmingham.

Scene from *All God's Chillun Got Wings* (1946), with (l-r) Robert Adams, Sydney Keith, Joyce Heron, Tim Duggan, and Edric Connor. Pauline Henriques, later in John Elliot's TV docu-drama, *A Man From the Sun* (1956), made her debut in this TV show.

Most of the roles that black and Asian actors did get were in sitcoms about racial tension, such as *Love Thy Neighbour* (with Rudolph Walker), *Fosters* and *Curry and Chips*, rather than quality drama. As Norman Beaton said, no-one in the industry was writing quality parts for black and Asian people. Michael Abensett's *Empire Road*, the first black soap with a predominantly black cast, which ran for two seasons between 1978 and 1979, was an important step forward. For the first time, ordinary life among black people in Britain – stories about human relationships and family conflict – was explored without the filter of racial tension.

The largely self-financed black films of the 1960s, such as Lloyd Reckord's *Ten Bob in Winter*, Lionel Ngakane's *Jemima and Johnny* and Horace Ove's *Baldwins Nigger* and *Reggae* never reached mass audiences. Ove's *Pressure*, which was produced with the Trinidadian writer, Sam Selvon, in 1975, was banned for three years, and was the first black feature film to be made in Britain. It was only in the 1980s that films such as *Young Soul Rebels*, *The Passion of Remembrance* and *Handsworth Songs* were screened in central London for a wider audience. In 1986, Horace Ove was awarded the British Film Institute's Independent Film and TV Award for his 'contribution to British culture'.

The turning point came in 1981 when the British Film Institute gave Menelik Shabazz a grant to make *Burning an Illusion*. It marked the beginning of an era of funding polices that were to dominate ethnic minority film development for the next ten years. The establishment of Channel Four in 1982, with a mandate to cater for minority interests and tastes, set the seal on it.

Whereas the BBC's *Apna Hi Ghar Samajhiye*, an English language educational series broadcast in 1965, had been about providing a 'service' for black and Asian audiences, Channel Four's *Black on Black* (produced by Trevor Phillips) and *Eastern Eye* (produced by Samir Shah) – to which the BBC responded with *Ebony* and later *Network East* –

were intended as programmes that reflected ethnic minority interests. The appointment of Farrukh Dhondy as commissioning editor for multicultural programming at Channel Four took these initiatives further, and programmes such as *Bandung File, The Black Bag* and *Doing It With You...Is Taboo* were produced. New sitcoms were commissioned – *No Problem*, by Farrukh Dhondy and Mustafa Matura, and *Desmonds* by Trix Worrell – and film-making was encouraged by funding film and video workshops such as Ceddo, Black Audio Film Collective, Retake and Sankofa. It gave us films such as Sankofa's *Territories,* written by Isaac Julien, and the Black Audio Film Collective's *Handsworth Songs* by John Akomfrah.

Lenny Henry, who made his name as a TV comedian.

In the 1990s, second generation writers and film makers from Britain's ethnic minorities are bringing new perspectives to old questions about the representation of Britain's ethnic minorities. Hanif Kureishi's filmscripts for *My Beautiful Launderette* – which won the Evening Standard Award for the Best Film in 1985 – and *Sammy and Rosie Get Laid*, became big box office successes. Meera Syal, already well-known for her three-part series for the BBC, *My Sister Wife*, wrote the filmscript for *Bhaji on the Beach* (1993), the first feature film directed by a British Asian woman, Gurinder Chadha; Harwant Bain's *Wild West*, which won the Critics' Award at the Edinburgh Festival in 1992, told the story of a Pakistani country and western band and its young Southall hero; and Ninder Billing's *Movin' as a Massive*, a short film, won the Lloyds Bank Bafta Award in 1994.

Trevor MacDonald was *not* the first black man to present Britain's news; in the 1950s, Cy Grant sang the news in calypso to British TV audiences every night. However, the real integration of ethnic minority presenters into news and current affairs programmes only came in the 1980s when Moira Stuart and Connie Chang began to present the news. Now we also have Zeinab Badawi on *Channel Four News,* Shahnaz Pakravan on *Tomorrow's World* and, of course, Trevor MacDonald on ITN's *News at Ten;* Andi Peters, Diane Louise-Jordan and Derek Griffiths are familiar children's television presenters; Trevor Phillips is a frequent host on the *The Midnight Hour* on BBC 2; Ben Okri debates life and death on *The Brains Trust;* Darcus Howe plays *Devil's Advocate* on topical issues such as 'transcultural adoption' and teenage girls' magazines; *Panorama*'s Martin Bashir has made his name forever by interviewing Princess Diana; Chrystal Rose is Britain's answer to Oprah Winfrey; and George Alagiah, Krishnan Guru-Murthy, Anya Sitaram and Matthew Amroliwalla report regularly on developments in South Africa, Bosnia, Northern Ireland, the latest local

David Yip, as *The Chinese Detective*.

The cast of *Desmond's*, a TV sit-com which stars Norman Beaton (centre) as the proprietor of a hairdressing salon.

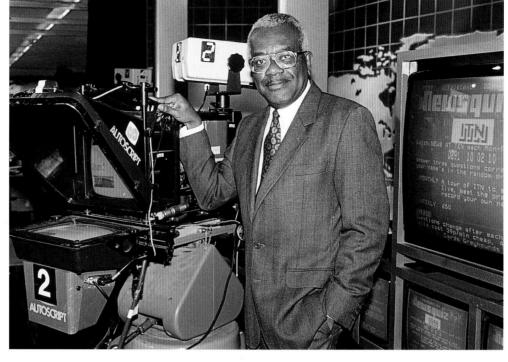

▶

Trevor MacDonald's career as news presenter on ITN's *News at Ten* brought him a government invitation to head a commission on improving national standards of written and spoken English.

Zeinab Badawi, presenter of *Channel 4 News*.

▼

▶

Emeric Pressburger, the emigré producer who, together with director Michael Powell, was responsible for many highly acclaimed films of the 1940s and 1950s, including *The Life and Death of Colonel Blimp*, and *The Red Shoes*.

elections in Britain, or issues such as moonlighting and tax evasion, which Dilip Bhattacharya from the University of Leicester has calculated to cost the UK £85 billion a year. Television actors from ethnic minorities include Patrick Robinson (cousin of football player Ian Wright) as a member of the *Casualty* team; Jaye Griffiths as a crimebuster in *Bugs*; and Colin Salmon as Detective Sergeant Bob Oswalde in the award-winning *Prime Suspect II*.

Behind the scenes, Beverley Randall is one of the producers of Channel 4's series *The Posse*; Alan Yentob, director of programmes for BBC radio and TV, is of Iraqi Jewish descent; Samir Shah, who came to the UK as an eight-year old from India, is now Head of Political Programmes for BBC television and radio; and Michael Grade is chief executive of Channel Four. One of Grade's uncles was the famous Jewish impresario, Sir Lew Grade, the moving force behind over a quarter of a century of ITV program-

ming, while another, Lord Delfont, became chairman and chief executive of EMI Films and Theatre Corporation.

Jewish involvement in the film and cinema industry has been extensive since the war. Sir Michael Balcon was executive producer of two of Britain's leading cinema production companies, Gaumont British Picture Corporation and Gainsborough Pictures. He was also executive producer at Ealing Studios, and responsible for the Ealing comedy series produced between 1938 and 1959, which gave us masterpieces such as *Kind Hearts and Coronets* and *The Lavender Hill Mob*. Oscar

◄

Meera Syal with Paul Bhattacharya, in BBC TV's *My Sister Wife*, written by Syal.

Deutsch began the Odeon cinema chain, and Lord Sidney Bernstein, son of a Swedish immigrant, was the architect of Granada TV.

Two of Britain's most prolific film producers were immigrants. Alexander Korda, who came to Britain with his brothers Zoltan and Vincent from Hungary in 1931, produced classics of the British cinema such as *The Third Man,* scripted by Graham Greene, and containing the famous Harry Lime tune; *The Thief of Baghdad*; and *Richard III* (with Laurence Olivier). Emeric Pressburger, a German immigrant, worked with Michael Powell to produce *The Life and Death of Colonel Blimp* and *The Red Shoes.*

Early BBC radio recordings show the remarkable change that has also taken place in radio broadcasting. The BBC, like the other channels, now actively tracks down diverse regional accents, and recruits from all ethnic groups. Where once only Christians could have a *Thought for the Day*, today we hear from members of all creeds, and both sexes; Rabbi Julia Neuberger and Rabbi Lionel Blue are regulars on the programme, as well as many others. Rabbi Hugo Gryn makes life difficult for his interviewees on the panel of *Moral Maze*, while Jenny Abramsky has risen to be head of Radio 5. Paul Gambaccini, who came to Britain from the USA, spent 18 years at

STARS OF STAGE AND SCREEN

Actors today move from theatre to television and film with equal ease. Actors from every ethnic minority group have made their reputations in both media.

NAVEEN ANDREWS

SUDHA BHUCHAR

ELEANOR BRON

JEANNE CAMPBELL

NADIA CATTOUSE

MARTY FELDMAN

PETER FINCH

HENRY GOODMAN

BARRY HUMPHRIES

JUDITH JACOB

MIRIAM KARLIN

BEN KINGSLEY

SUSAN LEONG

RULA LENSKA

MAUREEN LIPMAN

ART MALIK

MIRIAM MARGOLYES

ZIA MOHYEDDIN

WOJTEK PSZONIAK

COLIN SALMON

ROSHAN SETH

ANTONY SHER

JOSETTE SIMON

VICTOR SPINETTI

DAVID SUCHET

CATHY TYSON

PETER USTINOV

RITA WOLF

Saeed Jaffrey settled in London in 1966 after a spell in New York where he worked with Laurence Olivier. He joined the BBC World Service, but made his name in films for the big screen such as David Lean's *A Passage to India*, and Hanif Kureishi's *My Beautiful Launderette*, plus countless television dramas such as *Tandoori Nights*, *Rumpole of the Bailey*, and *Little Napoleons*.

Radio 1, and was a presenter for Classic FM and Radio 3. Programmes such as Tanika Gupta's four-part series, *Pankhiraj*, on Radio 4, are now a regular feature of radio broadcasting in Britain today.

The wealth of 'ethnic' radio stations – such as Avtar Lit's Sunrise Radio, and Choice FM, which began broadcasting in 1990 as Britain's first 24-hour soul music station – and the continual incorporation of 'ethnic interests' into mainstream programming, for example Radio 1's jungle, reggae, rap and soul shows, with Lisa I'Anson as the first daytime black woman presenter – cannot leave any doubt that Britain today speaks in many voices, languages and accents.

Lisa I'Anson, once of Kiss FM and MTV, now one of the voices of Radio 1.

A voice of the future: a BBC Radio trainee.

Rabbi Lionel Blue, a regular on Radio 4's *Thought for the Day*.

LITERATURE AND PUBLISHING

▲

Joseph Conrad was born to a Polish family in the Ukraine in 1857, and fulfilled a childhood dream when he became a sailor at 16. He became a British subject in 1886, but only settled here after 20 years at sea. He started writing in English, his third language (after Polish and French), when he was 38. He is best known for novels such as *Lord Jim*, *Nostromo*, *The Secret Agent*, and *Heart of Darkness*, on which the film *Apocalypse Now* was based.

Many writers have described themselves as 'outsiders', and have said that creative work calls for a sense of detachment. This could explain why immigrants, who are by definition 'outsiders', at least for some time after they arrive, are drawn to the profession. In 1991, 3,300 (22%) of the 14,800 ethnic minority cultural workers in Britain described themselves as 'authors, writers or journalists', making it by far the largest category. Pakistanis, Bangladeshis and Indians were most likely to belong to this group.

When George Lamming from Barbados and Sam Selvon from Trinidad arrived in Britain in 1950, they spent their first years in a state of culture shock. Even though they had been educated in British schools, read Shakespeare and the great Victorian novelists, and knew all about team spirit and 'fair play', real British culture had little in common with the packaged variety they knew. Selvon wrote of the coldness, not just of the weather, but the people – 'it have people living in London who don't know what happening in the room next to them, far more the street or how other people living ...' he said; while Tornado, a character in Lamming's *The Emigrants* gave his fellow travellers on the boat from Port-of-Spain the benefit of his knowledge of England in almost identical words:

> ... in England nobody notice anybody else. You pass me in the street or sit next to me in the train as if I come from a next planet. If yuh hungry you keep it to yuhself and if yuh rich the same thing. Nobody ask questions and nobody give answers. You see this the minute you put foot in London. The way the houses build was that people doan' have nothing to do with one another. You can live an' die in yuh room an' the people next door never say boo to you no matter how long you inhabit that place.

Novelists and poets such as Caryl Phillips (who has also written filmscripts), Joan Riley, Merle Collins, Timothy Mo, Ravinder Randhawa, Buchi Emecheta, Wallace Collins, Grace Nichols and many others – write about the sense of being caught between two worlds, the feeling of being outsiders in Britain. Mike Phillips (also a journalist and scriptwriter) has created, in Samson Dean, the first black British sleuth. Hanif Kureishi, author of *The Buddha of Suburbia* and *The Black Album*, emphasises that he is British and that Britain is where he belongs, for better or worse. The playwright, Winsome Pinnock, saw her play, *Mules,* co-produced by Clean Break Theatre Company and the Royal Court Theatre in June 1996.

Like C L R James, who declared that he could not accept the system of values whereby two famous social historians of England could 'between them never once mention the man [W G Grace] who was the best-known Englishman of his time', some of the recent immigrants have used their writing to question the cultural preconceptions they have encountered. For example, Kazuo Ishiguro's novel, *The Remains of the Day*, set in Lord Darlington's home in deepest English countryside, explores how 'things that had been thought about as the highest patriotic achievements suddenly turned out to be something dreadful.'

The Booker Prize was set up in 1969 and is awarded to the best full-length novel written by a citizen of the UK, Eire or the Commonwealth and published in the UK. Just under half of the 28 Booker prize winners since 1969 were born outside Britain. They include V S Naipaul, from Trinidad, for *In a Free State*, who also won the David Cohen Literature Prize, awarded for a lifetime's work, and was knighted in 1990;

MY FIRST LANGUAGE

My first language:
A relief, a comfortable secret
Helping me, hindering me,
Making me a stranger.

My second language:
Powerful.

Two strange languages
inside my head.

JUAN BERGANINOS FUENTES
(15 years old, Pimlico School, 1981)

WORDS OF PASSAGE

A selection of some of the words English has borrowed from other languages
(not including Latin, Greek, French and other Western European languages)

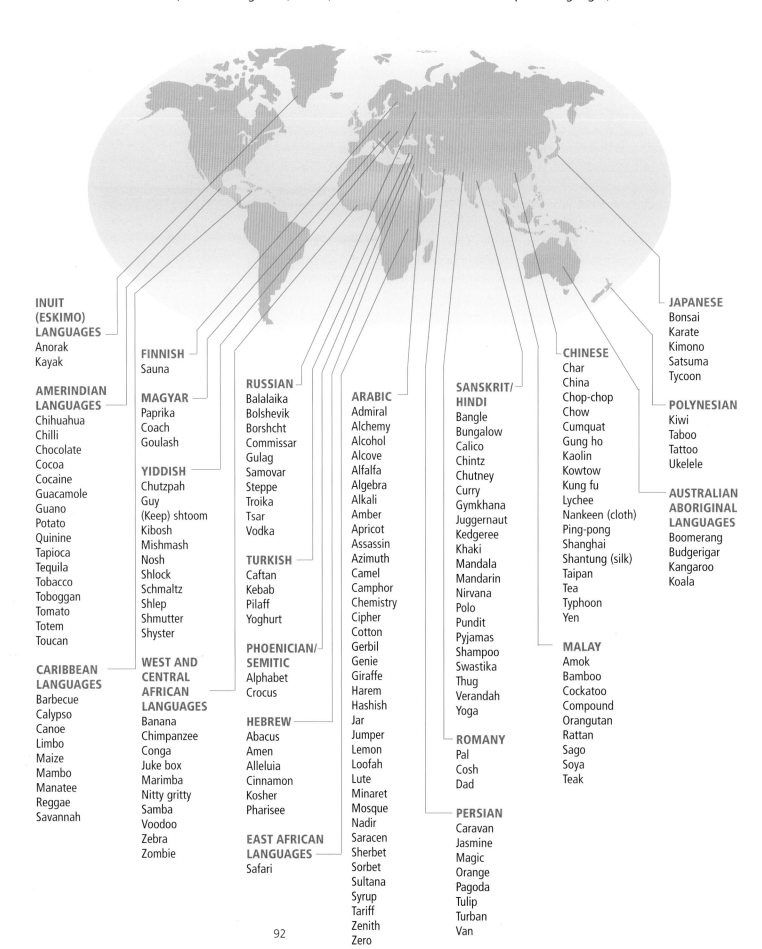

**INUIT
(ESKIMO)
LANGUAGES**
Anorak
Kayak

**AMERINDIAN
LANGUAGES**
Chihuahua
Chilli
Chocolate
Cocoa
Cocaine
Guacamole
Guano
Potato
Quinine
Tapioca
Tequila
Tobacco
Toboggan
Tomato
Totem
Toucan

**CARIBBEAN
LANGUAGES**
Barbecue
Calypso
Canoe
Limbo
Maize
Mambo
Manatee
Reggae
Savannah

FINNISH
Sauna

MAGYAR
Paprika
Coach
Goulash

YIDDISH
Chutzpah
Guy
(Keep) shtoom
Kibosh
Mishmash
Nosh
Shlock
Schmaltz
Shlep
Shmutter
Shyster

**WEST AND
CENTRAL
AFRICAN
LANGUAGES**
Banana
Chimpanzee
Conga
Juke box
Marimba
Nitty gritty
Samba
Voodoo
Zebra
Zombie

RUSSIAN
Balalaika
Bolshevik
Borshcht
Commissar
Gulag
Samovar
Steppe
Troika
Tsar
Vodka

TURKISH
Caftan
Kebab
Pilaff
Yoghurt

**PHOENICIAN/
SEMITIC**
Alphabet
Crocus

HEBREW
Abacus
Amen
Alleluia
Cinnamon
Kosher
Pharisee

**EAST AFRICAN
LANGUAGES**
Safari

ARABIC
Admiral
Alchemy
Alcohol
Alcove
Alfalfa
Algebra
Alkali
Amber
Apricot
Assassin
Azimuth
Camel
Camphor
Chemistry
Cipher
Cotton
Gerbil
Genie
Giraffe
Harem
Hashish
Jar
Jumper
Lemon
Loofah
Lute
Minaret
Mosque
Nadir
Saracen
Sherbet
Sorbet
Sultana
Syrup
Tariff
Zenith
Zero

**SANSKRIT/
HINDI**
Bangle
Bungalow
Calico
Chintz
Chutney
Curry
Gymkhana
Juggernaut
Kedgeree
Khaki
Mandala
Mandarin
Nirvana
Polo
Pundit
Pyjamas
Shampoo
Swastika
Thug
Verandah
Yoga

ROMANY
Pal
Cosh
Dad

PERSIAN
Caravan
Jasmine
Magic
Orange
Pagoda
Tulip
Turban
Van

CHINESE
Char
China
Chop-chop
Chow
Cumquat
Gung ho
Kaolin
Kowtow
Kung fu
Lychee
Nankeen (cloth)
Ping-pong
Shanghai
Shantung (silk)
Taipan
Tea
Typhoon
Yen

MALAY
Amok
Bamboo
Cockatoo
Compound
Orangutan
Rattan
Sago
Soya
Teak

JAPANESE
Bonsai
Karate
Kimono
Satsuma
Tycoon

POLYNESIAN
Kiwi
Taboo
Tattoo
Ukelele

**AUSTRALIAN
ABORIGINAL
LANGUAGES**
Boomerang
Budgerigar
Kangaroo
Koala

Salman Rushdie, who was born in India, for *Midnight's Children* – he also won the Booker of Bookers, a special award made in 1993 to mark 25 years of the Prize; Ben Okri, from Nigeria, for *The Famished Road*; Kazuo Ishiguro, who was born in Japan and came to Britain when he was four, for his third novel, *The Remains of the Day* – his second, *An Artist of the Floating World* won the 1986 Whitbread Prize; and Ruth Prawar Jhabvala, a Polish refugee to Britain, for *Heat and Dust*. Anita Brookner and Bernice Rubens are from the British Jewish community. Among others who have made it to the shortlist are Abdulrazah Gurnah, Caryl Phillips, Timothy Mo and Romesh Gunneskara.

Ethnic minority writers have also been prominent among winners of other literary awards. James Berry won the 1981 National Poetry Prize for *Fantasy of an African Child*; Fred D'Aguiar was awarded the 1994 Whitbread Prize for *The Longest Memory*; David Dabydeen received the Commonwealth Prize for Poetry in 1984 for *Slave Song*, written in Creole; Caryl Phillips won the James Tait Black Memorial Prize for *Crossing the River*, which was also shortlisted for the Booker Prize; and Amit Chaudhuri, from India, won the 1992 Commonwealth Writers Prize for Best First Book for *A Strange and Sublime Address*, and the 1993 Southern Arts Literature Prize for *Afternoon Raag*.

The long presence of Irish people in Britain has produced many exceptional writers, but it is sometimes difficult to distinguish between Irish writers and Anglo-Irish writers. For example, Sean O'Casey, who came to Britain in 1926 and spent the rest of his life here, appears to be regarded as an Irish playwright who just happened to live here. There is less ambivalence about playwrights such as Richard Brinsley Sheridan, who created Mrs Malaprop in *A School for Scandal*, and who, as an MP, became actively involved in British politics and culture; or John O'Keefe, author of the highly successful play, *Wild Oats*, who came to London from Dublin in 1780, 'determined to follow the trumpet of Fame and the rattling music of Fortune's purse ...'. George Bernard Shaw and Oscar Wilde, too, spent most of their lives in England, and were active in the social, political and literary movements of their time.

Robert Noonan, better known as Robert Tressell, was born in England in 1897, and worked as a house painter for a builder in Hastings. His novel, *The Ragged Trousered Philanthropists*, which is about a year in the lives of a group of workers in Mugsborough, was published in 1914 after he died of tuberculosis in Liverpool. William Trevor, who was born and educated in Ireland and lives there most of the time, writes about misfits, wanderers and transients, and his stories, like *Fools of Fortune* and *Felicia's Journey*, are often set in both Ireland and England. Among numerous others are Maeve Binchy, Edna O'Brien and J O'Donoghue.

The East End of London was home to some of Britain's best-known playwrights and poets. Isaac Rosenberg was born in Bristol in 1890 and moved to Whitechapel with his family seven years later. His father was a scholarly man, but worked as a pedlar and market dealer. In 1911, another Jewish family paid for Isaac to go to the

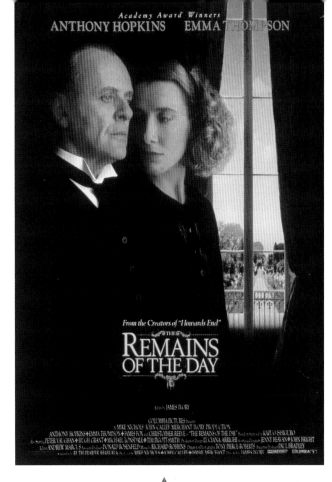

▲

Japanese-born Kazuo Ishiguro's novel, *Remains of the Day*, won a Booker prize and was made into an Oscar-winning film by Merchant Ivory Productions. The novel sold over one million copies in English alone – Ishiguro's work has been translated into 22 languages.

An East End-born Jew, Stephen Berkoff is well-known as an actor, director and writer.

▶

◀

A scene from Tom Stoppard's play *Rosencrantz and Guildenstern are Dead*. Stoppard was born in Czechoslovakia in 1937, brought up in Singapore and came to Britain after his father died. Other Stoppard plays include *The Real Inspector Hound*, *Travesties* and *Arcadia*.

Slade School of Art, and a year later he published *Night and Day,* encouraged by the poet, Ezra Pound, and others. He was killed in the trenches in 1918. Siegfried Sassoon, too, enlisted in the war, but survived to publish his war poems. Three contemporary East End writers are Arnold Wesker, Harold Pinter and Steven Berkoff – it is probably true to say that one of their plays is in rehearsal or production somewhere in the country every day of the year. Pinter and Berkoff are also very successful directors and actors. Other well-known Jewish authors include Elaine Feinstein, Willy Goldman, Simon Blumenfeld, Bernard Kops, Gabriel Josipovici, Anita Brookner, Clive Sinclair, Peter Shaffer, and Ralph Glasser. Like other ethnic minority writers, some of them write about belonging; the essential migrant identity of Jewish people as a 'wandering tribe'; and the ambivalent feelings they have towards Europe, which they see both as the source of Jewish intellectual tradition and as a place of nightmare.

George Orwell once remarked that the most striking fact about English literature during this century is the extent to which it has been dominated by 'foreigners'. Two US immigrants were among the most influential literary figures of the century. Both became British subjects. Henry James lived here for 20 years, and was awarded the Order of Merit in 1916. He was a prolific writer of novels such as *The Portrait of a Lady*, *The Spoils of Poynton, The Ambassdors,* and *The Wings of the Dove,* as well as travel sketches and critical essays. Thomas Stearns Eliot came from Missouri in 1914, taught briefly at Highgate School and worked for Lloyds Bank for eight years. He was director of Faber and Faber, the publishers, and was awarded the Nobel Prize and the Order of Merit in 1948. Ezra Pound, another US poet, best known for his *Cantos,* spent 12 years in Britain between 1908 and 1920. Elias Canetti, a Spanish Jew from Bulgaria escaped to Britain from Nazi Europe in 1938. His greatest works are *Auto da Fé*, published in 1935 before he came here as *Die Blendung,* and *Crowds and Power*, published in 1985. Canetti was awarded the Nobel Prize for Literature in 1981. The University of Leeds was where another future Nobel Prize winner, Wole Soyinka, studied in the 1950s. He was a playreader at the Royal Court Theatre in London, where his plays *The Swamp Dwellers, The Lion and the Jewel* and *The Invention* were produced. He returned home to Nigeria in 1960. Jung Chang, who came to Britain in 1978, became the first person from the People's Republic of China to receive a doctorate from a British university. Her novel, *Wild Swans*, topped the bestseller list. She now teaches at London University. George Mikes, a Hungarian immigrant, is the author of *How to be an Alien,* and *Eating People is Wrong.* Ranjit Bolt's decision to give up his job as an investment manager has given us a long string of very fine new translations of French and German plays, such as Bertolt Brecht's *The Resistible Rise of Arturo Ui*, Molière's *Tartuffe* and *The Miser*, and Rostand's *Cyrano*.

Publishing has always been a source of employment for writers and intellectuals, and many refugees and immigrants, including students from the Empire, set up their own houses or established new journals. Duse Mohammed Ali's *African Times and Orient Review* was a political forum for Africans in Britain mobilising around the question of national independence. Others such as Krishna Menon and James Tambimuttu, no less committed to their political causes, had other interests as well. Both were responsible for introducing the English reading public to the work of some of its most celebrated authors. Menon, who was appointed editor of the new Pelican series by Allen Lane, chose George Bernard Shaw's *Intelligent Woman's Guide to Socialism* to launch the series in 1937. Tambimuttu, who was born in Sri Lanka, stayed in Britain long enough to set up a new journal in 1939, *Poetry (London)*, which published work by W H Auden and Marghanita Laski.

Carmen Callil from Australia was one of the founders of Virago Press, established to publish new writing by women and to recover texts that had gone out of print. Naim Atallah, a Palestinian, set up Quartet Books when he came to London, and introduced the English reading public to European writers such as Ryszard Kapuscinski and Juan Goytisolo. Arif Ali's Hansib Publishing, Jessica and Eric Huntley's publishing house Bogle L'Ouverture and their Walter Rodney Bookshop – one of the first black bookshops in London – and John La Rose and Sarah White's New Beacon Books provided opportunities for ethnic minority authors in Britain as well as writers from developing countries. Hansib Publishing, set up in 1971, was for many years Britain's largest publishing house run by and for the country's 'non-white' ethnic minorities, while John La Rose also organises an annual Third World Bookfair, with international speakers.

Two relatively recent ethnic minority publishing houses are Steve Pope and Dotun Adebayo's XPress and Maxim Jakubowski's Mask Noir. Jakubowski, son of a Polish Jew who served with the British forces during the Second World War, spent his childhood in France. He returned to Britain in his twenties, and started up Virgin Books for Richard Branson before setting up the UK's first specialist crime bookshop, Murder One, in London's Charing Cross Road.

Many of Britain's most distinguished publishers came here as refugees from Germany or central Europe where Jews had been involved in publishing for years – Andre Deutsch, Paul Hamlyn, Ernest Hecht (Souvenir), Walter Neurath (Thames and Hudson), George Weidenfeld, and Bela Horowitz (Phaidon). Robert Maxwell, a refugee from Czechoslovakia, included among his enterprises

▲

Naim Atallah, Palestinian author and chairman of the publishing firm, the Namara Group, owns Quartet Books, The Women's Press, *Literary Review*, *Wire* magazine and The Academy Club.

an agreement with a German publisher to issue scientific journals in Britain, the establishment of Pergamon Press, and the Mirror Group of newspapers. Victor Gollancz, grandson of a Jewish immigrant who arrived in the middle of the nineteenth century, set up the well-known publishing house as well as the Left Book Club in 1936.

The national press in Britain has been dominated by immigrants, notably Canadians. Max Aitken, who became Lord Beaverbrook, acquired the Express Newspaper Group and the *Evening Standard* in the1950s. Roy Thomson launched his career with the purchase of Scottish Television in 1956, followed by *The Sunday Times* in 1959 and *The Times* eight years later. He was made a peer in 1964. Conrad Black has been chairman of the Telegraph Newspaper Group since 1987. Eddie Shah, of Asian origin, launched *Today* in the 1980s – it closed down in 1995 long after he had sold it – and Australian-born Rupert Murdoch's company, News International, owns four national newspapers.

Claudia Jones established the Brixton-based *West Indian Gazette* in 1958.
▼

Many immigrant groups, especially those who spoke a different language when they arrived, published community newspapers and journals, often in their own languages, but also in English. One of the earliest, the *West Indian Gazette*, was established just after the 1958 Nottingham riots, when Claudia Jones, a Trinidadian-born immigrant from the USA, saw the importance of a newspaper to bind the community together. She produced the paper until her death in 1964. She is buried next to Karl Marx in Highgate Cemetery in London. Mahmood Hashemi, a Pakistani journalist who became a teacher when he came to Birmingham in the late 1950s, realised that, with little news about Pakistanis in Britain or about the countries of the Indian subcontinent, there was scope for a community paper. He set up *Mashriq* (East). By the late 1960s there were nine Indian language weeklies, including one of the oldest, *India Weekly*. After the war, scores of Polish newspapers were produced, both in Polish and Yiddish. *Dziennik Polski* (The Polish Daily) was the only Polish language daily published in Europe outside Poland, and has been going for half a century, although its circulation has dropped since 1935, when it sold 35,000 copies a day.

Today, hundreds of dailies, weeklies, monthlies and specialist magazines and journals are produced by ethnic minority publishers in a variety of languages including Urdu, Greek, Turkish, Arabic, Gujarati, Bengali, Turkish, Chinese, Hindi, Italian, Japanese, Punjabi, as well as English. They conduct vigorous debates about British and international politics, and provide an invaluable service for their own communities. Of the English language papers, the *Jewish Chronicle*, which was first published in 1841, *The Irish Post*, set up in the early 1970s, and *The Voice*, a black newspaper, have circulation figures of about 50,000 or more.

As well as the ethnic minority journalists and editors working for these publications, there are many with prominent positions in the mainstream press. A full list would probably be as long as this book, but it would certainly include, from *The Observer*, Polly Ghazi and Melanie Phillips; from *The Guardian,* Vivek Chaudhary, Anita Chaudhuri, Angella Johnson, Gary Younge and Maya Jaggi; from the *Independent on Sunday,* Kenan Malik and Neil Ascherson; from the *Daily* and *Sunday Telegraphs,* Amit Roy and Dominic Lawson; from *The Times,* Bernard Levin; from *The Financial Times*, Samuel Brittan; from *Women's Realm*, Kathy Watson; and freelancers, Yasmin Alibhai-Brown, Vikram Dodd, Dilip Hiro, Germaine Greer and John Pilger.

ART AND ARCHITECTURE

ew ideas and styles are never assimilated more quickly than when they become part of our everyday environment. The traditional Paisley pattern is derived from the Kashmiri tear-drop design and is as English as chintz, a printed calico from India. In the nineteenth century, Augustus Pugin's neo-Gothic style, which found its fullest expression in the church of St Giles in Cheadle, Staffordshire, radically transformed British taste in furniture and interior decoration, while the influence of Italian architecture can be seen in a number of eighteenth century Palladian villas. The mosaics on the floor of the Bank of England were laid by Italian craftsmen, and the mosaic murals adorning Tottenham Court Road underground station in London were created by Eduardo Paolozzi, the Scottish-born son of Italian immigrants. In Birmingham, the sculpture for the fountain in Victoria Square was carved by Druva Mistry, of Indian origin, who became the youngest Royal Academician since Turner in 1991.

Sir Jacob Epstein, a Russian Jew who emigrated to Britain in 1904 from New York, created a huge controversy with his sculptures for the frieze of the British Medical Association building, then in the Strand, and his memorial to Oscar Wilde (now in the Père Lachaise cemetery in Paris). They were branded 'immoral' and elicited loud, but unsuccessful, calls for their removal. George Bernard Shaw was one of his champions. Epstein went on to do work for the Festival of Britain, the new Coventry Cathedral, Llandaff Cathedral in Cardiff, the Trades Union Congress memorial to the war dead, busts of Bertrand Russell, Albert Einstein, and much more. He was knighted in 1954.

Much less controversial were the sculptures contributed to the Albert Memorial by the Irishman, John Henry Foley, one of the most popular Victorian sculptors. He was responsible for the figures of the Prince Consort and 'Asia', while his compatriots, Patrick Macdowell and John Lawlor, produced 'Europe' and 'Engineering' respectively. The architect, Berthold Lubetkin, a Russian immigrant, designed the penguin pool at London Zoo, which was built in 1934, as well as the animal pavilion at

▲
Druva Mistry's sculpture in Victoria Square, Birmingham.

◄
A mosaic at Tottenham Court Road Underground station by Eduardo Paolozzi. Born in Edinburgh of Italian immigrants, Paolozzi was interned with his family when Italy declared war against Britain in 1940. His father was one of the internees being deported to Canada on the ill-fated *Arandora Star* in July 1940 when it was torpedoed by a German U-boat and sunk. 700 lives were lost; 486 of the victims were of Italian origin.

Berthold Lubetkin's penguin pool at London Zoo.

Zaha Hadid in front of her Vitra fire station.

Sir Jacob Epstein's *St. Michael Fighting the Devil*, at Coventry Cathedral. His spare and angular work was initially denounced by the art establishment, but he is now acknowledged as one of the masters of modern sculpture.

Whipsnade Zoo, the Pine Street Health Centre in Finsbury, and Highpoint, the apartment block in north London. Zaha Hadid, an architect from Iraq, studied at the Architectural Association in London. Her design for the Cardiff Bay Opera House won first prize, but the opera house may never be built, due to lack of funds. Hadid was also shortlisted for the Victoria and Albert Museum's extension.

In the sixteenth century, there was a firm belief at the English court that only artists who had established their reputations abroad were any good. As well as the several court painters brought in from Europe, there were innumerable visitors and students, many of whom stayed. Marcus Gheeraerts, who is credited with the Ditchling portrait of Elizabeth I, came to London in 1567; Wenceslas Hollar was a Bohemian engraver, whose work included many images of seventeenth century London; and François Roubilliac, a French Huguenot sculptor who arrived in the first half of the eighteenth century. Apart from his bust of Handel, for which he received 300 guineas, Roubilliac was responsible for two splendid memorials in Westminster Abbey: to Field Marshal George Wade, and to Lady Elizabeth Nightingale. The well-known painter of London scenes, Antonio Canale (called Canaletto) was a Venetian who spent a lot of time in London between 1746 and 1755, painting views of the city. More than a century later, the French impressionist painters Camille Pissarro and Claude Monet helped to make the Thames one of the most familiar rivers in the world. Giambattista Cipriani, a Florentine artist, designed the gold state coach made for George III in 1762 and used for coronations ever since. An Italian patriot, Gabriele Rossetti, who came to Britain in 1824, was the father of the Pre-Raphaelite poets, Christina Rossetti and Dante Gabriel, who was also a painter, and whose work can be seen at the Tate Gallery.

Some of the leading artists of this century came here as refugees during the two World Wars, or are the children of refugees. Frank Auerbach, one of the children rescued at the last minute from Nazi-occupied Europe, and Leon Kossoff, a Russian Jewish immigrant at the beginning of this century, were taught at the Borough Polytechnic by the painter David Bomberg, also the son of Polish Jewish immigrants. Bomberg was one of the founders of the London Group, but did not receive the recognition he deserved in his lifetime. Josef Herman OBE was born in Warsaw and came

Camille Pissarro (1831-1903) produced this painting of Crystal Palace in 1871. Like his fellow artist, Claude Monet, he was a refugee from the Franco-Prussian War.

to Britain in 1940, living in Glasgow first and then in Ystradgynlais in Wales. His drawings of miners won him a gold medal from the Royal National Eisteddfod for services to Wales. Herman later also painted the women at Greenham Common, whom he greatly admired. Feliks Topolski, a refugee from Warsaw in 1935, spent the years between 1940 and 1945 as a war artist. The murals in the lobby of the Carlton Tower Hotel in London are by him. Topolski was awarded the Gold Medal of Honour by the Fine Arts Council in 1955. Kurt Schwitters, who belonged to the Dadaist movement, was a refugee from Germany in 1940. He created a retreat for himself in Ambleside in the Lake District, where he experimented with the art of collage. His work has been called the egg out of which British pop art was hatched. Schwitters' British citizenship came through the day before he died. The modernist architect, Erno Goldfinger, a Hungarian Jewish refugee in 1934, designed his own house in Hampstead, which has just been purchased by the National Trust.

Several US artists have settled in Britain: James McNeill Whistler, who came to

Tea Room, a drawing by the Polish refugee, Feliks Topolski (1904-1989).

'A Music Hall', by Walter Sickert, a painter of Danish origin, who inspired the Camden Town school of painting.

Mark Gertler's 'Pomegranates and Handkerchief'. Gertler was born in Spitalfields, London, in 1891, to Polish Jewish parents. He spoke only Yiddish until he was eight. Assisted by the Jewish Educational Aid Society and numerous scholarships and prizes, he studied at the Slade School from 1908-1912. Gertler became a member of the London Group, and held his first one-person exhibition in Paris in 1921. He killed himself in June 1939 in London.

London in 1859, was a leading figure in what was called the 'aesthetic movement'. He was strongly influenced by Japanese prints and would have known the work of Yoshio Markino, the Japanese water colourist and author of *A Japanese Artist in London*, who spent 44 years in London. Another US immigrant, John Singer Sargent, came to London via Florence in 1885, and painted numerous portraits – of Roosevelt, Rockefeller, Chamberlain, and Lord Ribblesdale; the French sculptor, Rodin, called him 'the Van Dyck of our times'. R B Kitaj, a figurative artist, is a more recent Jewish immigrant from the USA. He came to Britain on an art scholarship in 1958, and has become increasingly interested in Judaism since his study of the Holocaust. Some of his paintings are in the Tate Gallery.

Walter Sickert once said of himself: 'No-one could be more English than I am. Born in Munich in 1860 of pure Danish descent.' Sickert studied under Whistler, and was greatly influenced by the Impressionist painters in France. He inspired the Camden Town school of painting – it was where he spent most of his life. His paintings can be seen in the Tate Gallery, the British Museum and the Manchester City Gallery.

Some ethnic minority artists have had to contend with a tendency to judge their work on the basis of cultural assumptions about, say, 'Indian', 'African' or 'Oriental' art, similar to those that were made about 'Italianness' in the eighteenth century. The painter, Avinash Chandra, who came to England from India in 1955, was speechless when a gallery owner asked him if he painted elephants and tigers. Chandra might well have painted elephants and tigers if he had put his mind to it, but he did not, as can be seen in the Tate Gallery, the Victoria and Albert Museum, and the Arts Council collection where some of his works are displayed.

Francis Newton Souza, who came to London from India in 1949, dominated the British art scene between 1956 and 1966. He represented Britain at the Guggenheim International Awards in New York in 1958, and his work can be seen at the Victoria and Albert Museum, and the Tate and National Galleries in London. The paintings of Namba Ray, the late Indian painter, are also on display in the National Gallery.

Ronald Moody (brother of Harold Moody), was born in Jamaica in 1900, and came to London in 1923 to study dentistry. He drifted into philosophy, and a wrong turning in the British Museum led him to his vocation. He graduated from plasticine to oak, concrete and fibreglass, aluminium, copper and glass resin. In 1977, he was awarded the Musgrave Gold Medal, Jamaica's most prestigious cultural award, 'for his eminence as an international sculptor', and the Minorities Rights Award in 1981, 'for an outstanding contribution to sculpture in Britain'. The serene dignity of Moody's work was given its full due in the words of a Dutch critic who called him 'one of the greatest sculptors today ... a master from the moment he begins to work in wood'. Moody died in London in 1984.

In 1989, the work of all these artists as well as other ethnic minority artists living and working in Britain were brought together in a major exhibition at the Hayward Gallery in London called *The Other Story*. They included David Medalla, born in the Philippines; Gavin Jantjes, from Cape Town; Aubrey Williams, a black painter who died in London in 1990; and Li Yuan Chia, a Chinese artist who also died recently. The exhibition was curated by Rasheed Araeen, who came to Britain from Karachi in 1964 as a civil engineer, and turned to sculpture in 1968. He has played an important role in promoting the work of ethnic minority artists, and started an art journal, *The Third Text*, in 1987.

Artists from a newer generation, most of them born in Britain, include Sonia Boyce, Eddie Chambers and Keith Piper. Their work often deals with the question of belonging, and the experience of racial

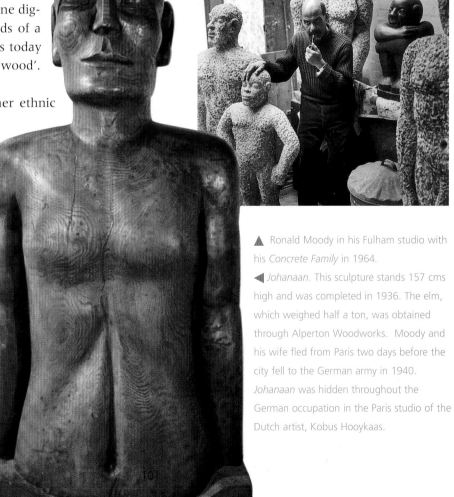

Charles Saatchi in his London gallery. Saatchi came to London from Baghdad in 1947 when he was four years old. He began collecting contemporary art in the late 1960s and, with his brother, developed what became the biggest advertising agency in the world in the 1970s. His idea for advertising Silk Cut cigarettes – a piece of purple silk with a cut in it – doubled the company's market share, while the agency's image of a queue of unemployed workers with the slogan 'Labour isn't working', helped to persuade people to vote for the Conservative Party in 1979. In 1985 he opened the Saatchi Gallery in London to house what Nicholas Serota, director of the Tate Gallery, has called 'the finest collection of contemporary art in the world.'

▲ Ronald Moody in his Fulham studio with his *Concrete Family* in 1964.

◄ *Johanaan*. This sculpture stands 157 cms high and was completed in 1936. The elm, which weighed half a ton, was obtained through Alperton Woodworks. Moody and his wife fled from Paris two days before the city fell to the German army in 1940. *Johanaan* was hidden throughout the German occupation in the Paris studio of the Dutch artist, Kobus Hooykaas.

Anish Kapur's *To Reflect an Intimate Part of the Red* (1981). Kapur won the Turner Prize for his sculpture in 1991.

The Carrot Piece, by Lubiana Himid, who was born in Zanzibar. It was included at *The Other Story* exhibition at the Hayward Gallery in London.

Permindar Kaur. *Untitled, February 1994.*

and ethnic difference in Britain. Boyce was born in east London in 1962 to a Barbadian mother and Guyanese father. Together with photographer David A Bailey she is now curator of the African and Asian Visual Art Archive. Mona Hatoum, who has lived in Britain since 1975 when she was forced to leave Beirut, was a contender for the Turner Prize in 1995. Anish Kapur, from Bombay, won the Turner Prize in 1991 for his work as a sculptor, and the prestigious Premio Duemila Venice Biennale in 1990. He declined to exhibit his sculpture at *The Other Story*, because he did not want it to be seen as 'ethnic art'. Permindar Kaur, who was born in 1965 in Nottingham, works in glass, steel and clay, and sees her art as an experiment with form. Her work was shown at the 1995 British Art Show.

The explosion of printed images in magazines, newspapers and advertisements is a measure of the extraordinary power the press has to impose identities on people, as well as to control what we see. A number of photographers such as Zarina Bhimji, Suzanne Roden, Vanley Burke, David A Bailey, Mumtaz Karimjee, Sutapa Biswas, and Sunil Gupta use photography to challenge the way people from ethnic minorities are represented by the western media, as well as to break new ground in photography.

In 1991, 4,300 out of 14,800 ethnic minority cultural workers in Britain said they were working as architects, artists, commercial artists and graphic designers. Including 300 industrial designers and 600 clothing designers, this area accounted for 35% of all ethnic minority cultural workers.

Immigrants and ethnic minority artists have been central to the shaping and making of British art in several ways. They have added to the body of art produced in and for Britain and British people, and extended the range of major national collec-

tions such as those at the Tate Gallery, the Victoria and Albert Museum, the National Gallery and the Arts Council. They have also contributed to Britain's understanding of itself as a multicultural society, and to its international reputation as a rich centre of contemporary art.

INTELLECTUALS AND SCHOLARS

oreign inventors, thinkers and scholars have always played a central role in Britain's creative and intellectual life, but the arrival of emigrés from the continent in the nineteenth century hit Britain like an intellectual hurricane. The idea that 'colonial subjects' could teach Britain anything, however, would have been unthinkable to the vast majority of British people. Yet it was students from the Empire, schooled in the writings of the European Enlightenment and the poetry of Shakespeare and Milton, who held up the country's best intellectual traditions as a mirror to imperial realities. When Learie Constantine and C L R James toured Lancashire, they smuggled the case for West Indian self-government into talks about W G Grace, and found supporters for both. Krishna Menon's single-handed, seven-year battle against dominion status for India (which was won), and the subsequent campaign for *swaraj* (self-rule), persuaded influential men such as Bertrand Russell, Fenner Brockway, J B S Haldane, Stafford Cripps and George Hicks of the justice of his cause, and shaped the ideas and policies they subsequently went on to develop in their respective fields. As a Labour MP, Fenner Brockway, for example, tenaciously submitted Bills to outlaw racial discrimination every year from 1951 onwards.

▲

C L R James, Trinidadian historian, campaigner for social justice and cricket enthusiast. His best-known books are *Black Jacobins* and *Beyond a Boundary*.

Like many asylum-seekers before them, the intellectuals, scholars and scientists from Nazi-occupied Europe who found refuge in Britain more than repaid the country for giving them shelter. Not only were they extraordinarily productive as intellectuals and scholars, but many worked at the heart of Government, influencing policy. The two Hungarian refugees, Nikolaus Kaldor and Thomas Balogh, became distinguished theoretical economists, advisers to the Wilson government and, eventually, peers of the realm. Sir Claus Moser, from Germany, was former Head of the Central Statistical Office, where he was responsible for the annual audit, *Social Trends,* and former chairman of the Royal Opera House. Sir Nikolaus Pevsner, a German art historian, spent five years at the Dresden Gallery before he came to Britain. He was Slade Professor of Fine Art at Cambridge and Professor of the History of Art at Birkbeck in 1955. He was appointed editor of King Penguins, and published the well-known series, *The Buildings of England* and *The Englishnesss of English Art*. Pevsner died in 1983. Sir Lewis Namier, a historian, was born in Poland to a Jewish family, and became deeply involved with the plight of Jewish refugees during the 1930s, and with Zionism. Sir Karl Popper, the Austrian philosopher of science, found refuge in New Zealand before coming to Britain in 1945. He taught at the London School of Economics, and published books such as *The Logic of Scientific Discovery* and *The Open Society and its Enemies*. The Viennese art historian, Sir Ernst Gombrich, served with the

Sir Isaiah Berlin OM, political philosopher and historian of ideas (standing). He moved with his parents from his birth place in Latvia to Russia, where he witnessed both the social democratic and Bolshevik revolutions before coming to Britain.

Sir Karl Popper, Austrian philosopher of science and author of *The Logic of Scientific Discovery* and *The Open Society and its Enemies*.

Professor Shula Marks OBE came to Britain in 1960 from South Africa. A historian who has researched and written extensively on the history of South Africa, Professor Marks was Director of the Institute of Commonwealth Studies from 1983-93. She is currently Professor of History of Southern Africa at the School of Oriental and African Studies in London. She is also Chair of the Society for Protection of Science and Learning, which assists refugee academics in Britain.

BBC Monitoring Service during the war. He is Director of the Warburg Institute, Emeritus Professor at the University of London, author of the very popular *The Story of Art*, and was awarded the Order of Merit in 1988. Sir Isaiah Berlin, the distinguished political philosopher and historian of ideas was a Latvian Jew. He was awarded the Erasmus Prize, the Jerusalem Prize for civil liberties and the Order of Merit in 1971.

Numerous other 'foreign-born' scholars and intellectuals have contributed to British academic and intellectual life, among them Ludwig Wittgenstein, who studied the philosophy of mathematics under Bertrand Russell at Cambridge and published only one work, *Tractatus Logico-Philosophicus* in 1922. By 1930, plagued by doubts about his theory, he abandoned philosophy altogether. George Gilbert Murray arrived in Glasgow from Australia in 1899, and is best known for his verse translations of classical Greek plays. He was chairman of the League of Nations between 1923 and 1938, and was awarded the Order of Merit in 1941. Arthur Lewis, author of *Economic Survey 1919-1939*, which is still regarded as a classic, became the first black Professor of Economics at a British university, before joining the University of the West Indies, and then Princeton University in the USA. He was knighted, and won the Nobel Prize for Economics in 1979.

Preliminary analysis of the 1992/3 Labour Force Survey shows that 16% of British university professors were born overseas. Like ethnic minority academics born in the UK, they are spread across all the disciplines, from science and medicine to cultural studies; and work as teachers, professors, lecturers and researchers. Many have published extensively, and are internationally respected in their field. Ralf Dahrendorf, former Director of the London School of Economics, now Warden of St Antony's College, Oxford, is the author of the 1995 report, *Wealth Creation and Social Cohesion*. Stuart Hall, who has played a leading role in the development of cultural studies in Britain, came to Oxford from Jamaica as a Rhodes Scholar in English. He was one of the founder members of the journal, *New Left Review,* and became Director of the Centre for Contemporary Cultural Studies in Birmingham, set up by Professor Richard Hoggart. Hall is now Professor of Sociology at the Open University. Homi Bhabha, a Parsi from Bombay, who taught at the University of Sussex, is another leading scholar in this area. Lord Meghnad Desai, from India, is Professor of Economics at the London School of Economics. Eric Hobsbawm, the historian, was born in Egypt, and taught history at Birkbeck College, London until his retirement. Bhikhu Parekh, originally from India, is Professor of Politics at the University of Hull. He was a former Commissioner and deputy chairman of the Commission for Racial Equality. Raphael Samuel is Professor of History at Ruskin College, Oxford. Akbar Ahmed is a Fellow of Selwyn College, Cambridge, and Dr Zaki Badawi, from Egypt, is Principal of the Muslim College.

Britain's colleges and universities continue to attract overseas students. In 1992, there were 85,000 overseas students in the public sector, and nearly half a million in the private sector, in all fields of study. The estimated contribution to the 1990 gross domestic product was £1,167 million, or 4% of British export earnings.

The resources that individual ethnic minority communities have accumulated about their own histories and culture are an invaluable addition to the intellectual and cultural wealth of the country, and provide unique archives of Britain's own history and changing culture. The Polish Social and Cultural Centre (POSK), set up in 1974 in Hammersmith, London, boasts an art gallery, a bookshop, a theatre, and the unmatchable Polish Library with over 100,000 books, 40,000 photos, 5,000 periodical titles and hundreds of manuscripts. Supporting it are the Polish Institute and the Sikorski Museum in Kensington, the most comprehensive resource in Europe on Polish involvement in the Second World War. The Chinese Chamber of Commerce in London's Soho has established the largest Chinese language school in Europe with nearly one thousand pupils. The Bharatiya Vidya Bhavan and the Nehru Centre provide venues for artists, visiting performers, lectures, exhibitions, and other educational events. And there are the London Museum of Jewish Life, the Manchester Jewish Museum, the Africa Centre, the Irish Centre, the Islamic Cultural Centre, and many more.

▲

Bhikhu Parekh, Professor of Politics at the University of Hull.

FAITHS AND BELIEFS

There is perhaps greater religious diversity in the UK today than in any other country in the European Union. Christians of many denominations make up the largest group. There are also substantial communities of Hindus, Jews, Muslims and Sikhs, and smaller groupings of Bahai's, Buddhists, Jains and Zoroastrians, together with many other kinds of formal and informal religious expression and non-religious and humanistic beliefs and philosophies.

Precise statistics on the faith communities are not available, since Britain does not presently include a question about religion in its census. *Religions in the UK: A multi-faith directory* discusses the statistics problem and, based on the few information sources that were available in 1993, gives estimated figures as: Baha'i 6,000; Buddhist 130,000; Christian 37.6 million; Hindu 400,000; Jain 30,000; Jewish 300,000; Muslim 1.5 million; Sikh 400,000; Zoroastrian 6,000. A number of these figures are now likely to be higher.

WORSHIP AND CELEBRATION

Britain's changing skyline reflects this growing diversity of faith. Churches, chapels and synagogues have been joined by increasing numbers of gurdwaras, mandirs, mosques, temples and viharas. A few mosques and gurdwaras were built in the early years of this century, for example the Shah Jehan mosque in Woking, the first mosque to be built in the UK in 1900, and the gurdwara in Putney, the first to be opened in 1911. When the new communities settled in Britain, their first places of worship were often converted buildings such as redundant churches, old factories or modified houses. Now, alongside these, are many beautiful purpose-built places of worship such as the Central Mosque in Regent's Park, London, and the recently opened Swaninarayan Hindu Temple in Neasden, London.

Each faith has its own holy days and festivals, and these are often celebrated

▲
The Greek Orthodox church in Wood Green, north London, is a centre of worship for the local Greek-Cypriot community. A Greek Orthodox church was built in London as early as 1677.

▶

Christian worship in Coventry.

106

publicly in multi-faith cities such as Leicester, with special decorations and processions in the streets. Because the various faiths follow different calendars and have their celebrations at different times, there are few times of the year when there is not a religious date of significance to one or other community. The festivals are described and explained in an annual calendar produced by the Shap Working Party on World Religions.

Regent's Park Mosque, London. The first mosque in Britain, the Shah Jehan Mosque in Woking, Surrey, was built in 1900.

Jewish children in Bradford watch the lighting of Hanukah candelabra.

Sikh women celebrating Baisakhi in Southampton.

The Swaminarayan temple in Neasden, north London was opened in 1995.

DIVERSITY WITHIN COMMUNITIES

Within most of the faith communities there is unity of basic beliefs, but also considerable diversity of ethnic background and cultural traditions, as well as interpretation of aspects of their religious heritage. Because of the variety of backgrounds, it is important not to confuse 'ethnicity' with 'religious affiliation', although there can of course be considerable overlap. To take Buddhism as an example, there are many groups from its two historical strands: Mahayana and Theravada. The majority of Chinese, Japanese and Vietnamese Buddhists belong to Mahayana groups, while Burmese, Sri Lankan and Thai Buddhists in Britain are usually linked to Theravada viharas. All groupings also now have followers from ethnic groups indigenous to Britain.

Other faith communities vary to a greater or lesser degree in background. Britain's Muslim population, for example, embraces the Sunni tradition and the smaller Shi'a tradition, and counts among its members people from the wide variety of ethnic groups that make up Britain today: English, Welsh, Irish, Scots, Caribbean, Cypriot, East African, Indian, Iranian, Malaysian, Arab, Turkish and Pakistani. While the Sikh population is more homogeneous, coming predominantly from the Punjab, the Hindu population encompasses people of Gujarati, Punjabi and other origins in the Indian subcontinent as well as a number of indigenous followers, and expresses its beliefs and practices in a wide variety of ways.

Christians are among the most diverse of Britain's faith communities. Among the traditions represented in the UK are:

Anglican, Baptist, Congregational, Methodist, Moravian, Pentecostal, various Orthodox Churches, Presbyterian, Quaker, Roman Catholic, Salvation Army and United Reformed. Within most denominations, Christians of many different ethnic backgrounds are to be found, as they have been throughout British history.

FAITH COMMUNITIES AND PUBLIC LIFE

Faiths reflect and influence social, cultural and political events and movements. In Britain, 'meddlesome priests', dissenting clergy, and fiery preachers have infuriated monarchs and parliaments through the ages, sometimes paying with their lives. The Reformation of the sixteenth century and the Protestant churches which arose from it, provided a catalyst for revolutionary economic and social change. The Jewish community has also produced many important social reformers. Today members of many faiths add their voices to those seeking to shape a just and humane society reflecting the values of Britain's varied spiritual heritage.

Members of the various faiths in Britain have worked hard to encourage respect for each other. Since 1987 Britain's major faith communities and inter faith bodies have been linked by the Inter Faith Network for the UK which works with them to promote good relations between the faiths in this country. Among the numerous local inter faith groups are the Wolverhampton Inter Faith Group founded in 1974 and Leeds Concord Sharing of Faiths founded in 1976, two of the earliest groups.

◀

Celebrating the Chinese New Year, or Spring Festival, in London.

William Cuffay, Chatham-born grandson of a slave, was a tailor by profession and a leading member of the Chartist Movement. He chaired the committee which organised the march in 1848 to deliver the People's Charter to Parliament. Continued agitation led to his arrest and eventual transportation to Australia.

The Trinidadian Pan-Africanist, George Padmore, shared a flat, as well as political purpose, with C L R James while they were in London together. Padmore published *How Britain Rules Africa* in 1936.

SOCIAL JUSTICE

Many immigrants throughout history have been among the most socially and politically active citizens. As newcomers, they questioned things that local people took for granted. They were also aware that they had to negotiate terms of settlement. Even when they had been invited to Britain by its monarchs, with offers of special privileges, they were only outsiders as far as local people were concerned, and had to tread a fine line between deferring to tradition and forging a way through it. Most had to take whatever jobs were going, but it was never long before they felt sufficiently at home to challenge unfairness. The Russian and East European Jews achieved the feat of organising thousands of individual tailors and seamstresses into unions. Irish immigrants, led by men such as Ben Tillett and John Doherty, joined unions or helped to set them up. Black slaves and freemen such as Ignatius Sancho, Olaudah Equiano, and William Cuffay were tireless campaigners against the slave trade and social injustice. Students from the Empire such as George Padmore worked closely with Fenner Brockway and Reginald Reynolds of the 'No More War Movement' in the 1930s, and Sophia Duleep Singh, the Indian suffragette, was prominent in the fight for votes for women. Others such as Richard Sheridan, Edmund Burke, Emmanuel Shinwell, Jayanti Saggar, John Archer, Chunilal Katial, Dadabhai Naoroji, Mancherji Bhownagree and Shapurji Saklatvala became councillors, mayors and Members of Parliament.

COMMUNITY ORGANISATION AND UNIONS

The post-war immigrants from the former Empire followed in these footsteps. Self - help and enterprise were their answer to the indifferent reception they got from many people in Britain. If confirmation were needed that local reactions to black people and Asians were more than an age-old suspicion of foreigners, a survey in 1975 by Political and Economic Planning found it when it reported that 17% of applications by Italians for white-collar work were rejected compared with 30% from equally qualified black and Asian applicants.

The first difficulty many new immigrants encountered was finding somewhere to live. In 1956, John Darragh, a British journalist, found through a private poll that only 15 out of 1,000 Birmingham people were willing to rent accommodation to coloured people. The immigrants met similar obstacles in business, education and elsewhere. Cut off, sometimes even barred, from social intercourse with local British people, West Indians and Asians began opening their own clubs, pubs, shops, places of worship, supplementary schools, newspapers, financial services and community organisations. Inevitably, the greater the social distance the British people kept, the stronger grew the

Sophia Duleep Singh, the Maharajah Duleep Singh's daughter, selling the *Suffragette* outside Hampton Court Palace, in 1913. Madame Cama was another Indian woman active in the suffragette movement.

bonds within the new communities.

Most British people did not know very much about 'West Indian' and 'Asian' cultures, which are far more diverse than these terms suggest. Guyanese, Trinidadians, Jamaicans, Barbadians and others from the region only became 'West Indians' after coming to Britain; while 'Asians' could be Sikhs, Hindus, Jains or Muslims, as well as Punjabis, Gujaratis, Kashmiris, or Bengalis; not to mention their national origins as Indians, Pakistanis, Bangladeshis, Ugandans, Kenyans or Sri Lankans. Quite how much accommodation and adjustment was actually going on was, therefore, seldom appreciated. When Punjabi Sikhs first arrived, only those who were fluent in English could find work in transport, and only if they shaved their beards and removed their turbans. Thousands of Sikhs, going against their religious convictions, removed their turbans and cut their hair to improve their chances of finding jobs; Muslims who were required to pray five times a day compromised by praying once a week, on Friday; and Hindus, Muslims, and Sikhs celebrated their holy days at weekends if they fell on weekdays.

The accommodation was not one sided. Many British employers also cooperated by adjusting work breaks to suit fasting patterns. Leicester education authority waived the school uniform for Muslim girls, and Manchester Transport Committee allowed Sikhs to wear turbans in the colour of the uniform. However, there were as many stories of intransigence, both by employers and unions – in Bristol as we have seen, and elsewhere, where the transport committees adamantly refused to accept that turbanned men could punch tickets on a bus, even though they had driven tanks during the war without any mishap.

Community groups such as the West Indian Standing Conference, the Pakistani Welfare Association and the Indian Workers Association (IWA) with branches in Coventry and Southall, gave strenuous support to their members, trying to sort out bureaucratic problems and grievances at work, ranging from misunderstandings because of language to the degrading segregation of toilet facilities in some workplaces.

A succession of industrial disputes and strikes raised the same issues of differential pay and production targets for Asian and black workers throughout the 1960s and 1970s, sometimes without union support – at Courtauld's Red Scar Mill in Preston; at the Woolf Rubber Company in Southall; at Imperial Typewriters in Leicester; and at Coneygre Foundry in Tipton. At Mansfield Hosiery Mills in Loughborough, East African Asian women went on strike and took the company to an industrial tribunal for refusing to promote them to the skilled grades. They won.

The longest and best known strike led by ethnic minority workers involved East African Asian women at Grunwick Processing Laboratories in Willesden, London. The women made up 80% of all the employees. In 1976, Jayaben Desai and half the women stayed on strike for a whole year, trying to win recognition for APEX, the union they had just joined. The owner of the company was an Anglo-Indian. The strikers lost the battle, but won a moral victory in the support they received from

▲
Jayaben Desai led the year-long strike at Grunwick Laboratories, London, in 1976, to win recognition for the union.

▲
Bill Morris, the only black leader of a trade union, was elected general secretary of the T&GWU in 1992.

engineering, mining and building unions as it became clear that the women were defending the principle of the right to representation at work, irrespective of race or ethnic origin.

In other areas, such as hotels and restaurants, it was the lowest paid and most insecure migrants (many on work permits) who risked being sacked to win recognition for their union – in 1973, Turkish waiters and cooks in Wimpy Bars were getting 25p an hour for 100-hour weeks. The 1978 strike against Garners, where staff earned just £28 net for a compulsory 55-hour week, lasted 18 months. It was largely Cypriot community support that kept the strikers going.

As recently as 1995, a group of mainly Turkish and Kurdish workers at a frozen food distribution company in Tottenham, London, who had been locked out for joining a trade union, successfully pleaded unfair dismissal at an industrial tribunal. And at Hillingdon Hospital, Asian women went on strike against a cut in basic pay, and other penalties, when the hospital's cleaning and catering contract was privatised. The support from their communities, the hospital and the union, UNISON, was invaluable.

In 1989/90, 34% of all ethnic minority employees were members of trade unions, only 1% less than the overall average of 35%. But 44% of black employees and 38% of Indians were members of trade unions.

Cornelia Sorabji (top left), from a Christian Parsi family, at Somerville College, Oxford in 1889 where she was the first woman law student at a British university.

Refusal to accept discrimination and racial prejudice was not confined to the workplace. Vigorous campaigns were mounted against discriminatory policies in education, which the new immigrants prized above everything else for their children. Like Jews before them, they turned to their own resources. The black community set up supplementary schools modelled on the old Socialist Sunday Schools, while the National Muslim Educational Council, set up in 1979, served as an umbrella body for numerous local and regional Muslim educational organisations throughout the country.

Today, a significantly higher proportion of ethnic minority children are staying on at school, and going on to further and higher education, than the national average. This may be due in no small measure to their parents' efforts to ensure that their children get the full benefit of their dual cultural inheritance. In a world where people are increasingly employed on short contracts, and where business straddles the continents, the value of an international education, with the ability to speak several languages and communicate easily across different cultures, is becoming more widely recognised.

Over the years, a plethora of groups, alliances, committees and associations have formed and re-formed in response to the issues that have pressed on the changing communities of immigrants and their British-born descendants. The procession of immigration laws and rules which have cruelly divided families and served only to bolster racial prejudice and discrimination; excessive policing of ethnic minority areas; or racial harassment and physical violence against people from ethnic minorities, even today, as they go about the ordinary everyday business of their lives, have sparked vigorous opposition.

Sibghatullah Kadri QC took silk in 1989, while Her Honour Nasreen Pearce was the first Asian woman to become a circuit judge in 1994.

The Campaign against Racial Discrimination, one of the earliest expressions of common ground between organisations and individuals from all ethnic groups, the Indian Workers Associations, the Black People's Alliance, the Society of Black Lawyers, the Southall and Hounslow Youth Movements, Southall Black Sisters, the Irish Youth Foundation, Newham Monitoring Project, publishers and bookshops such as Bogle L'Ouverture, Hansib Publishing and New Beacon Books, educational bodies such as the Institute of Race Relations and the Runnymede Trust, advice agencies such as the Joint Council for the Welfare of Immigrants, collectives such as *Race Today*, racial equality councils throughout the country, and countless individuals associated with these or other groups, or representing themselves, have worked, and are still working, for social and racial justice in Britain, a justice which benefits not only ethnic minorities but British society as a whole.

Key players in the 1995 Scott Inquiry into arms sales included Christopher Muttukumaru (third from left), a civil servant and lawyer of Sri Lankan origin, and a specialist in European Union law. He was appointed secretary to the inquiry because of his knowledge of the Whitehall machine. Non-white ethnic minorities account for about one in twenty civil servants in Britain, most working at administrative levels. In 1995, they formed 2.5% of senior civil servants (Grades 1-7).

THE LEGAL PROFESSION AND THE JUDICIARY

Law was a popular subject among the students from the Empire, because of its relevance to the tasks their countries would face in writing constitutions and administering independent futures. The obstacles to full citizenship in Britain, and the need for legal expertise to challenge discriminatory policies and practices, have continued to attract large numbers of ethnic minority students to the law.

The first woman to study law in Britain was Cornelia Sorabji, a Christian Parsi. She studied at Somerville College, Oxford, and was awarded her degree in 1889. She could not be admitted to the Bar, not because of her ethnicity, but because she was a woman. Women were only admitted to the Bar in 1919, and only won the vote in 1928. It was as recently as 1988 that the black QCs Leonard Woodley and John Roberts took silk. Sibghatullah Kadri QC followed a year later, and Patricia Scotland became the first black woman QC to take silk in 1991. There are no Asian women QCs. After hundreds of years of Jewish settlement in Britain, Francis Goldschmid was the first Jew to be admitted to the Bar in 1843.

His Honour Judge Mota Singh became the first Asian circuit judge in 1982, the second was His Honour Judge Cooray, in 1991. Her Honour Nasreen Pearce was the first Asian woman to become a circuit judge in 1994. According to the Lord Chancellor's Department, there are another two 'other than white' circuit judges.

In 1993, 6% of practising members of the Bar were from non-white ethnic minorities. Nearly all the Bar committees in England and Wales had black and Asian barristers, and there were ten black and Asian QCs. However, three-quarters of the barristers practised in 19 predominantly ethnic minority chambers. There were 18 assistant recorders or recorders from ethnic minority groups.

A special interest in discrimination law began long before the present Race Relations Act was passed in 1976 – the Society of Black Lawyers was set up in 1973. Since then lawyers from all ethnic groups have done pro bono work for clients who have been turned away by other practices, and some have also set up multiracial chambers. In 1995, 4% of practising solicitors in England and Wales were from ethnic minorities.

LOCAL AND NATIONAL POLITICS

The students who came to Britain from the Empire were among the brightest from their countries – articulate, politically aware, and passionate believers in the 'rights of man' and national independence. Many got involved in local politics. Krishna Menon, who became India's defence minister and High Commissioner to London, was a

Home Rule for India and the good of St Pancras were the two commitments of Krishna Menon's life while he was in Britain. He was first elected to St Pancras council in 1934, and was returned with increased majorities at each subsequent election, so great was his popularity. In 1955, Camden Council conferred on Menon the Freedom of the Borough.

▼

Sir Dadabhai Naoroji was the first Indian professor of mathematics and natural philosophy, and president of the Indian National Congress for three sessions after it was formed in 1885. He came to Britain as a partner in Cama & Co. He was elected Liberal candidate for central Finsbury in 1892 by a majority of five votes. He lost his seat in the 1895 swing to the Tories.

CENTRAL FINSBURY

PARLIAMENTARY ELECTION, 1895.

D. NAOROJI.

Address to his Fellow Electors
in Central Finsbury, July, 1895.

devoted St Pancras councillor for 14 out of the 25 years he lived in Britain. It was one of his talks to a small audience of Unitarians in a Walthamstow church hall that 'awakened the MP Reginald Sorensen to the moral significance of India's cause'. The photographer, John Archer, born in Liverpool to an Irish mother and a Barbadian father, became Britain's first black councillor in 1906, and its first black mayor (of Battersea) in 1913. He was also the election agent in Sir Shapurji Saklatvala's successful campaign to represent Battersea North in 1922. Chunilal Katial became the first Asian mayor in Britain in 1938. In Dundee, a Punjabi doctor, Jayanti Saggar, was Scotland's first Asian councillor. He served the city for 18 years until his death, and the Lord Provost paid him this tribute: 'No son of Dundee had greater love for its people or worked harder in their interest.'

The new immigrants to Britain after the war were drawn into local politics gradually, as their numbers increased and their voice in local affairs became stronger. The number of ethnic minority councillors in Greater London trebled in 1985 from 60 to 200, with positive consequences for local services to their communities. It is estimated that there were about 600 ethnic minority councillors in Britain in 1995. Linda Bellos in the London Borough of Lambeth, Merle Amory in the London Borough of Brent and Bernie Grant in the London Borough of Tottenham were the first ethnic minority leaders of councils in Britain. Shreela Flather was the first ethnic minority woman councillor in Britain in 1976, and became the first Asian Lady Mayor for the Royal Borough of Windsor and Maidenhead in 1986. Mee Ling Ng, born in Malaysia of Chinese extraction, is among very few Chinese councillors. She has been a Lewisham

LONDON, TUESDAY, NOVEMBER 11, 1913.

'BLACK' MAYOR
OF
BATTERSEA.

SPEECH IN DEFENCE
OF HIS COLOUR
AND RACE.

WORLD'S RECORD.

John Richard Archer, Britain's first black councillor and mayor – of Battersea – was born in Liverpool in 1863. He was a photographer by profession, and was elected first president of the African Progress Union.

Sir Shapurji Saklatvala, Britain's third Asian MP, came here as a representative of the Tata company in 1905. His passionate support for working people was returned in full measure: a letter-writer to the *Daily Graphic* on 30 October 1924 proclaimed: 'I met a Battersea charwoman yesterday who was almost in tears because she lived on the wrong side of the street and could not vote for Sak ...'

councillor since 1986, and is currently deputy leader of the Council.

The chief obstacle preventing Jewish people from entering Parliament was the requirement to take a Christian oath. Lionel de Rothschild had been elected five times before a special Parliamentary resolution finally allowed him to take his seat in 1858. The Parliamentary Oaths Act was passed in 1866 removing the requirement. Disraeli took his seat in 1837 – he was baptised a Christian – and became prime minister in 1868, and again between 1874 and 1876. The first woman MP to take her seat was Nancy Astor, who was from the USA.

In 1871, Sir David Salomons MP introduced a Bill to enable Jewish businesses to stay open on Sundays and employ Jewish workers, provided they were shut on the Jewish Sabbath. It was a huge breakthrough and meant that Jewish proprietors could trade for the same number of days as others. At the end of the last century, the scandalous exploitation of Italian chimney sweeps and organ grinders was taken up by Anthony Mundella MP, son of an Italian political refugee, who introduced the Bill which subsequently became the Children's Protection Act 1889.

The first Asian Liberal MP, Sir Dadabhai Naoroji, a Parsi, was elected in 1892 by the constituency of Finsbury – although he first had to stand down charges of being 'a fire-worshipper and a black man'. Naoroji supported issues such as women's franchise, working men's clubs, trade unions, municipal reform and Irish Home Rule. His campaign to educate public opinion about British rule in India won support from men such as Keir Hardie and John Bright. Naoroji was followed by two more Parsi MPs: Sir Mancherji Bhownagree, who was elected Conservative MP for Bethnal Green NE in 1895, and Sir Shapurji Saklatvala (affectionately known as 'Sak' by working class supporters), who became Labour MP for Battersea North in 1922 and Communist MP with Labour Party support in 1924. Both Sir Bhownagree's election and Emmanuel Shinwell's in 1922, for Linlithgow constituency, were all the more impressive because both men were elected in constituencies with very few Asian or Jewish votes. All

◄

Sir Mancherjee Bhownaggree came into office in the swing to the Tories that unseated Sir Dadabhai Naoroji in 1895. Sir Mancherjee was re-elected in 1900, but lost in the Liberal landslide of 1905. He believed that British rule was good for India.

Benjamin Disraeli was Prime Minister of Britain in 1868, and again from 1874-1876. He wanted to be remembered for his novels. 'My works are my life', he once declared. His most famous novels are the trilogy: Coningsby, Sybil and Tancred.

▼

Lord Emmanuel Shinwell was elected MP for Linlithgow constituency in 1922.

▼

THE ROAD TO JEWISH EMANCIPATION

1656	'The Readmission': Jewish exclusion from the country ended by Cromwell.
1825	Jews allowed to naturalise as British citizens.
1830	Jews admitted to the freedom of the city.
1835	Francis Goldschmid becomes the first Jewish barrister.
1837	Jews win the right to graduate from London University.
1845	David Salomon, co-founder of Westminster Bank, is appointed Sheriff of the City of London.
1855	David Salomon becomes London's first Jewish Lord Mayor.
1858	Special parliamentary resolution allows Lionel de Rothschild to take his seat. He had been elected five times before.
1866	Parliamentary Oaths Act clears the way for Jews to enter Parliament without taking a Christian oath.
1871	Jews allowed to graduate from all British universities when requirement to take a Christian oath is lifted. Sir David Salomon's bill to legalise Sunday trading is passed.
1885	Lionel de Rothschild's son, Nathaniel, becomes the first Jewish peer.

Lord Pitt of Hampstead was made a peer in 1975, 19 years before he died. He came to Edinburgh as a medical student from Grenada and set up his own practice in Hampstead in 1947. He was one of the founding members of the Campaign against Racial Discrimination, and became President of the British Medical Association in 1985.

Diane Abbott MP for Hackney North and Stoke Newington, and Piara Khabra JP MP for Ealing, Southall.

Mark Hendrick MEP, Labour and Co-operative Party Member of the European Parliament for Lancashire Central.

Baroness Shreela Flather became the first woman councillor from a non-white ethnic minority group in 1976, the first Asian Lady Mayor for the Royal Borough of Windsor and Maidenhead in 1986, and the first Asian woman peer in 1990.

three Asians were dedicated constituency MPs, but Naoroji had been president of the Indian National Congress for three sessions and Saklatvala actively campaigned wherever and whenever he could against British rule in India and on behalf of the British working class – he was charged with sedition after he made a May Day speech in Hyde Park urging soldiers not to fire on workers. His commitment to their cause was not forgotten, and during the Spanish Civil War British volunteers fought in a Saklatvala Battalion.

It was more than six decades before Britain had another Asian or black MP. In 1970, David Pitt, the Grenadan doctor from Hampstead, became the first black candidate for Labour since the war, but he lost the safe seat of Clapham. In 1987, the four major political parties fielded 29 ethnic minority candidates. Keith Vaz, a Goan born in South Yemen, became Labour MP for Leicester East; Diane Abbott became the first black woman MP for Hackney North and Stoke Newington, the constituency that had elected David Pitt to the Greater London Council; Paul Boateng, a black barrister, won Brent South for Labour; and Bernie Grant became the Labour MP for Tottenham. All four were returned by constituencies with substantial ethnic minority populations.

In 1996, we have two additional Asian MPs: Piara Khabra (Labour), and Niranjan Deva (Conservative), elected at the 1992 general election. The Jewish community is well represented in the House of Commons, and there are several Jewish peers including the Chief Rabbi Emmanuel Jakobovits. Among the non-white ethnic minority peers, there are three Asians: Lord Pratap Chitnis, Lord Meghnad Desai and Baroness Shreela Flather, who became the first Asian woman peer in 1990. Since Lord Pitt's death in December 1994, there have been no black peers. Mark Hendrick is the only black British Member of the European Parliament.

Britain's six black and Asian MPs represent about 0.9% of the members of the House of Commons, which is far from being a microcosm of the nation. That is not to say that white politicians cannot, and do not, represent the interests of their ethnic minority constituents – there have always been numerous white people who have spoken out for a society that is free of racial discrimination and bigotry, and worked resolutely for equality of opportunity – but a democratic society cannot be truly representative – and seen to be so – unless its diverse elements represent themselves as well as others.

III

ROOTS
OF THE
FUTURE

ROOTS OF THE FUTURE

No-one today would deny the contributions the Huguenots have made to Britain's economic, technological and social development; nor the vital role the Jewish community has played throughout the history of their presence in Britain; nor the incalculable value of Irish labour going back a very long time. Yet in their own day, the activities of these migrants went unnoticed as achievements, and were, by and large, either taken for granted, or belittled and reviled. If this book had been written in the year 2096, the perspective of time would have shown just as clearly the essential role that the most recent immigrants to Britain have played, and are still playing, and the way they, and their descendants, are enriching its economic, social and cultural life. Looking at the present and trying to make sense of it is a bit like sitting in the front row of the cinema with one's nose up against the screen, unable to see it all at once and overwhelmed by the dizzying detail.

Facts and statistics can sometimes help to reveal the patterns in the weave, and to show how integral each strand is to the whole fabric. In Britain, however, unlike Germany or the USA, there are no statistics available demonstrating the role played by immigrants in the economy. Yet, as the British government itself acknowledged, immigrant labour was central to reconstruction and economic recovery. Even though the proportion of immigrants working in Britain was small, most of them were concentrated in a few key industrial sectors. Without them, manufacturing would have slowed down, there would have been even more bus and train cancellations, and the new National Health Service would have faltered even as it came into existence.

Their role today is equally vital. For example: 27% of London Underground's staff and over two-thirds of independently-owned local shops belong to ethnic minorities. About 23% of Britain's doctors, 15% of pharmacists, 13% of physiotherapists, 10% of nurses, 16% of university professors, 13% of travel agents, 10% of textile employees, 9% of hotel employees, 10% of domestic employees, 13% of service industry managers, and 24% of restaurant employees were born overseas. The influence ethnic minority musicians have had on British popular music is out of all proportion to their numbers in the population. And we can only be grateful that Britain does not have to play and run against Linford Christie, John Barnes, and Tessa Sanderson.

Yet this small, hard-working and highly productive population is still sometimes regarded as a 'problem', and the positive role it plays is either ignored or taken for granted. It is still claimed that 'they take our jobs', or that 'they are a drain on the economy', or 'a threat to British culture'. Not all immigrants inspire such concerns, however; just the ones who appear 'different', because of their race or colour, or the way they dress, or the fact that they speak other languages as well as English. With almost no primary immigration from the New Commonwealth countries in recent years, the persistence of such claims inevitably suggests that second and third generations of British-born, non-white ethnic minorities are also regarded as undesirable 'immigrants'.

All the evidence shows that, far from taking jobs from local people, the businesses that immigrants to Britain, and their descendants, have set up have *created* jobs, both for themselves and for other people. Their enterprise has contributed to an increase in the domestic market, and has had knock-on effects on other industries and services. In Birmingham there is now a clothing industry where there was none before, and in Manchester investments in textiles and clothing by the Pakistani community have helped to reduce imports. The expanding, new ethnic food sector, created and driven by immigrants and their descendants, was worth £1.5 billion in 1992, and employed 60-70,000 people. The higher rate of increase in international business activity between Britain and the countries from which some of its new settlers came after the war is partly a result of their own enterprising resourcefulness and the close contacts they have kept with families and friends in their original countries. The tourist industry, which depends so much on the labour and enterprise of Britain's ethnic minorities, particularly in London, is worth billions. In 1990, while 22% of UK nationals were in more highly paid – and taxed – professional or managerial jobs, 24% of immigrants from the European Union were in this group, and 28% of those from the 'rest of the world'. Meanwhile, young people from the second and third generations of Britain's 'non-white' ethnic minorities are more likely to stay on in education than on average – between 1988 and 1990, 53% of ethnic minority young people were in further and higher education, compared with 44% of the population overall.

More people have left Britain than entered it nearly every year since the 1960s, taking with them the education and skills that the nation has paid to develop. Judging from recent work permit figures, Britain still needs immigrants, particularly those with professional skills. Even with high unemployment and stringent immigration controls, there has been a steady rise in the number of work permits issued – in 1992, 52,000 work permit holders and their families – mainly from the USA and Japan – were permitted to enter Britain. In addition, of course, there are large numbers of people coming to Britain from Ireland and the European Union who do not need permits. As Allan Findlay, an economist, concludes, 'a very significant market demand for immigrant skills exists within the British economy.'

The fear that 'foreigners' might be a threat to British culture goes back centuries. Italian singers in eighteenth century Britain were warned in lampoons to 'Leave us as

we ought to be/ Leave the Britons rough and free.' Today there is a widespread belief that Britain only became a 'multicultural' society after the war; but Britain has never been an ethnically and culturally homogeneous society. The Celts would have had very little in common with the Saxons who tried to fight off the Norman invasion, and these, in turn, would have been strangers to the millions working in 'England's dark satanic mills' in the nineteenth century. Scots who visited Edward I's England were distinctly aliens, and in York in 1501 they had to use the hammers placed at the Bars to knock for admission.

From time to time, governments and monarchs have tried to close the nation to what they saw as corrupting outside influences, and to strangle all disagreement and dissent. The price has always been economic and cultural stagnation. In 1763, Peter Annet, a 70-year-old schoolmaster was imprisoned and stocked for translating Voltaire, and towards the end of that century Thomas Paine's *Rights of Man* was banned. Rational criticism and openness to new ideas have always been the basis of cultural renewal. In Britain, the struggle for civil and religious liberties in the eighteenth century, joined by dissenters of all descriptions and by liberal free traders, culminated in the breakdown a hundred years later of most of the old religious certainties – and the ideas of both Voltaire and Paine were finally absorbed into British culture. Japan's fantastic economic progress only came when it opened itself to the influence of other cultures, after two centuries or more of shutting itself off from the world.

Asked to say what British culture means, each of us would have a different answer, and we would come up with highly distinctive lists of 'essential' elements: thatched cottages, Christmas, Shakespeare, the Derby, and stuffed pheasant might be one version; jungle music, Arsenal, chicken kurma, Lenny Henry, and Joe Bloggs jeans another. In Calcutta or Lagos, inventories of 'essential' items that make up Bengali culture or Nigerian culture would be just as diverse, and they would be utterly different from those drawn up by the granddaughter of an immigrant to Britain from Calcutta or Lagos. No culture can be distilled into a few core elements without quickly becoming a misleading caricature. British culture has always been a rich amalgam of the thousands of sub-cultures and cross-cultures that are forever forming and re-forming. There is no 'single connecting thread' running through any culture that can package it meaningfully for all time.

Britain is a racially and ethnically diverse society. That counts for a lot in a world where national borders are becoming increasingly irrelevant. The ability to speak several languages, and to communicate across and between cultures is one of the most highly prized skills today. In classrooms throughout the country, young people from a wide mixture of backgrounds are picking up the languages and accents spoken around them, moving easily from Cockney to Patois or Punjabi, and arguing in them about the merits of Paul Ince over Paul Gascoigne, Oasis over Echobelly, *Trainspotting* over *Sense and Sensibility*. Young and old, we all take it for granted that when we treat ourselves to a meal out, we can choose between fish and chips, tandoori, stir fry, pasta or tapas, and that we have the same choices when we fill our trolleys at a supermarket. The difficulty of deciding whether to see the new Mike Leigh film, *Secrets and Lies*, or Adrian Lester in the musical, *Company*, may be enough to keep us at home twiddling our thumbs and tuning in to Trevor MacDonald for the *News at Ten*, or settling down for the evening with Hanif Kureishi's *The Black Album*. Britain's ethnic minorities are integral to what it means to live in Britain today. To speak of 'we' and 'they' is to deny our history.

If this book has in any way achieved its purpose, we shall have convinced our readers that, over the centuries, Britain has gained enormously from the skills, labour, capital, resourcefulness, and different ideas that immigrants and their descendants have contributed. We shall also have succeeded in showing that ethnic and cultural diversity is a good thing, and that it is nothing new in a country which, across its constituent nations, regions and social classes, has always contained wide variations of culture, belief, language, and accent. British culture is continually changing, through gradual mediations between these different indigenous cultural traditions, as well as those brought by the continual arrival of migrants throughout history. The cultures they have brought with them, themselves varied and richly textured, have likewise emerged in new forms, through the inevitable process of exchange, adaptation and synthesis in a new environment.

The past is where our roots lie, and we have much to learn from it. What we urgently need today is a sense of our histories and cultures as a shared past, one that brings together our diverse experiences and informs our understanding of the present. Only then can we take a full and active part in realising our vision of a shared future.

KEY DATES

500,000 BC	Earliest human presence in Britain – people come and go, according to the movements of the ice sheets.
25,000 BC	Britain connected to the continent at low tide.
6000 BC	Britain becomes an island, and people arrive by boat.
1,000–150 BC	Celtic-speaking peoples from central Europe cross the channel.
AD 43	Roman conquest begins – Roman soldiers drawn from all over Europe and North Africa.
410	Romans leave Britain. Invasions by Angles, Saxons, Jutes and Frisians.
871-1016	Intermittent Scandinavian migrations and invasions. Cnut accepted as King of England.
1066	William of Normandy conquers England.
1130	Merchants from Low Countries, Germany and Lombardy arrive as settlers.
1189-90	Massacres of British Jews.
1290	Jews expelled from Britain.
1337	Edward III invites clothworkers of all lands to England.
1507	Black trumpeter at Henry VII's court.
1554	Queen Mary marries Philip II of Spain – beginning of Spanish presence in Britain.
1555	First slaves brought to Britain – beginning of black presence in Britain.
1561	First settlement of Protestant refugees at Sandwich.
1598	The Steelyard is closed.
1600	East India Company granted charter.
1601	Elizabeth I orders Lord Mayor of London to expel London's small black population.
1630	First Asians brought to Britain as servants.
1656	Jews readmitted by Cromwell.
1660	Persecution of Huguenots begins in France under Louis XIV.
1681	Charles II offers sanctuary to Huguenots. About 40-50,000 refugees arrive in Britain.
1700s	Population of black and Asian slave servants and seamen increases
1707	Union of England, Wales and Scotland.
1736	Anti-Irish riots in London.
1753	Jewish Naturalisation Bill strongly opposed.
1765	Campaign for emancipation of slaves begins in Britain.
1783-8	British withdrawal from America brings loyalists to Britain, including small number of freed black slaves.
1780	Gordon Riots. Attacks on Catholic Irish. First records of Chinese sailors in London.

1789	Emigrés from French revolution come to Britain.
1801	Union of England, Scotland, Wales and Ireland.
1833	Abolition of slavery in Britain. Indentured labour from India and China used in the colonies and dominions.
1837	Queen Victoria's coronation.
1840	Queen Victoria's marriage to Prince Albert of Saxe-Coburg-Gotha brings more Germans to Britain.
1845-8	Famine in Ireland brings hundreds of thousands to Britain.
1848	Revolutions in Europe bring waves of emigrés to Britain.
1858	Emancipation of Jews in Britain. India brought under direct rule of the British Crown.
1881	Pogroms begin in Russia, and thousands of Jews flee to Britain.
1905	Aliens Act passed to reduce Jewish settlement.
1914-8	First World War. Influx from dominions, colonies and occupied Belgium. German businesses in Britain are confiscated and all German residents interned.
1920	Greek-Cypriot settlement begins.
1933	Hitler becomes Chancellor in Germany. Persecution of German Jews begins.
1936	Spanish Civil War brings refugees.
1938	Government tightens controls on emigrés.
1939	Second World War. Soldiers and workers from all over the Empire are stationed in Britain, including US troops, and 100,000 Poles fighting under British command. All Germans resident in Britain are interned or deported.
1940	Mussolini declares war against the UK on, 10 June and all Italians resident in Britain are interned or deported.
1943	There are 114,000 refugees in Britain.
1945	End of the war. Polish refugees and their families choose to settle in Britain.
1947	European Volunteer Workers Scheme introduced, to help with post-war reconstruction.
1948	*SS Empire Windrush* brings the first West Indian immigrants to Britain.
1950	Immigration from the Commonwealth begins. Encouragement of immigration from Ireland, West Indies, South Asia, Italy and Cyprus.
1962	Commonwealth Immigrants Act.
1968	British Asians are expelled from Kenya, and many settle in Britain.
1972	British Asians are expelled from Uganda, many settle in Britain.
1974	Turkish invasion of Cyprus brings refugees to Britain.
1976	Race Relations Act passed and the Commission for Racial Equality established. British Asians from Malawi settle in Britain.
1979	Vietnamese refugees arrive in Britain.
1981	British Nationality Act is passed.
1980s	Somali, Kurdish and Tamil refugees arrive in Britain.
1993	Asylum and Immigration Appeals Act is passed.

BIBLIOGRAPHY

Afro Hair and Beauty Industry, The Grapevine Press, 1995

Anwar, Mohammed, 'New Commonwealth immigration to the UK,' in *The Cambridge Survey of World Migration*, ed Robin Cohen, Cambridge University Press, 1995

Ali, Arif, *Third World Impact*, eighth edition, Hansib Publishing, 1988

Bagwell, Dr Phillip, *The Railwaymen: The history of the National Union of Railwaymen*, vols 1 and 2, George Allen and Unwin, 1963 (vol 1) and 1982 (vol 2)

Breughel, Irene, 'Unequal Outcomes: Ethnic minorities in the London labour market', South Bank University, forthcoming

British Tourist Authority, *Tourism: Digest of Tourist Statistics*, No 19

Brook, Stephen, *The Club: The Jews of modern Britain*, Constable, 1989

Bygot, David, *Black and British*, Oxford University Press, 1992

Coleman, David and John Salt, *The British Population: Patterns, trends and processes*, Oxford University Press, 1992

Commission for Racial Equality, *Working in Hotels: Report of a formal investigation into recruitment and selection*, 1991

Counter Information Services, *Hardship Hotel*, Report No 27

Dabydeen, David, *Hogarth's Blacks: Images of blacks in eighteenth century English art*, Dangaroo Press, 1985

Dabydeen, David, ed, *The Black Presence in English Literature*, Manchester University Press, 1985

Dear, I C B, ed *The Oxford Companion to the Second World War*, Oxford University Press, 1995

Department of Employment, *Employment Gazette*, January 1995

Department of Employment, *Employment Gazette*, June 1995

Department of Employment, *The Role of Immigrants in the Labour Market*, Report of the Institute of Manpower Studies, 1976

Department of Health, 'NHS hospital and community health services: non-medical staff in England,1983-1993', *Statistical Bulletin*, 1994/11, October 1994.

Department of Transport, *Bus Data*, 1996 edition

Department of Health, 'NHS medical, and dental staff in England 1984-1994', *Statistical Bulletin*, 1995/14, July 1995

Dummett, Ann and Andrew Nichol, *Strangers, Citizens, Aliens and Others: Nationality and immigration law*, Weidenfeld and Nicolson, 1990

Evans, Neil, 'Immigrants and minorities in Wales 1840-1990: A comparative perspective,' in *Llafor, Journal of Welsh Labour History*, Vol 5 No 4, 1991

Feist, Andy, *Overseas Earnings of the Music Industry*, British invisibles, 1995.

Feist, Andy and Jane O'Brien, *Employment in the arts and cultural industries: An analysis of the 1991 census*, Arts Council, November 1995.

File, Nigel and Chris Power, *Black Settlers in Britain 1655-1958*, Heinemann Educational Books, 1981

Findlay, Allan, 'An economic audit of contemporary immigration', in *Strangers and Citizens*, ed Sarah Spencer, Rivers Oram Press, 1994

Fishman, William J, *The Streets of East London*, with photographs by Nicholas Breach, Duckworth, 1979

Fryer, Peter, *Staying Power: The history of British people in Britain*, Pluto Press, 1984

Fuentes, Juan Berganinos, 'My first language', *City Lines*, Poems by London School Students, ILEA English Centre, 1982

General, Municipal and Boilermakers Union, *An Introduction to GMB Organisation in Hotel and Catering*, 1994

Graham-Dixon, Andrew, *A History of British Art*, BBC Books, 1996

Greater London Council, *London Industrial Strategy*, 1985

Greater London Council, *London Labour Plan*, 1986

Greater London Council, *The West London Report*

Harris, Nigel, *The New Untouchables: Immigration and the New World workers*, I B Tauris Publishers, 1995

Hiro, Dilip, *Black British, White British: A history of race relations in Britain*, Grafton Books, 1991

Holmes, Colin, ed, *Immigrants and Minorities in British Society*, George Allen and Unwin, 1978

Holmes, Colin, *A Tolerant Country? Immigrants, refugees and migrants in Britain*, Faber and Faber, 1991

Holzman, J M, *The Nabobs in England: A study of the returned Ango-Indian 1760-1785*, New York, 1926

Imperial War Museum, *Together: multi-media pack on the contributions made in the Second World War by African, Asian and Caribbean men and women*, 1995

James, Louis, *Print and the People 1819-1851*, Penguin Books, 1978

James C L R, *Beyond a Boundary*, Stanley Paul and Co Ltd, 1963

Jeyasingh, Shobana, 'Flexing the foot' in *Storms of the Heart: An anthology of black arts and culture*, ed Kwesi Owusu, Camden Press, 1988

Jones, Trevor, *Britain's Ethnic Minorities: An analysis of the Labour Force Survey*, Policy Studies Institute, 1993

Kay, D and R Miles, *Refugees or Migrant Workers? European Volunteer Workers in Britain: 1946-1951*, Routledge Kegan and Paul, 1992

Kipling, Rudyard, *The Works of Rudyard Kipling*, Wordsworth Editions Ltd, 1994

Kosmin, Barry, 'Exclusion and opportunity: trends of work amongst British Jews,' in *Ethnicity at Work*, ed Sandra Wallman, The Macmillan Press Ltd, 1979.

Lee, Robert, *Other Britain, Other British: Contemporary multicultural fiction*, Pluto Press, 1995

Lipman, V D, *History of the Jews in Britain since 1858*, Leicester University Press, 1991

Maan, Bashir, *The New Scots: The story of Asians in Scotland*, John Donald Publishers Ltd, 1992

Market Review, *UK Catering Market*, Keynote 95

Mayall, David, *English Gypsies and State Policies*, Gypsy Research Centre, University of Hertfordshire Press, 1995

Merriman, Nick, ed, *The Peopling of London: Fifteen thousand years of settlement from overseas*, Museum of London, 1993

Merrison, Dr Andrew FRS, Chairman, *Report of the Committee of Enquiry into the Regulation of the Medical Profession*, HMSO, 1975

Miles, Robert, *Racism and Migrant Labour*, Routledge Kegan and Paul, 1982

Modood, Tariq, 'The Indian economic success: A challenge to some race relations assumptions,' in *Policy and Politics*, vol 19 no 3, 1991

Morris, H, *We Will Remember: Jews in the armed forces*

Nicolson, Colin, *Strangers to England: Immigration to England 1100-1945*, Wayland Publishers, 1974

Oliver, Paul, *Black Music in Britain: Essays on the Afro-Asian contribution to pop music*, Open University Press, 1990

Orwell, George, 'In defence of English cooking,' *The Collected Essays, Journalism and Letters*, Vol 3: As I Please, 1943-1945, Penguin Books, 1968

Owen, David, *A Review of the 1991 Census and a Look Forward to the 2001 Census*, 1991 Census Statistical Paper No 11, Centre for Research in Ethnic Relations, University of Warwick, October 1991

Pines, Jim, *Black and White in Colour: Black people in British television since 1936*, British Film Institute, 1992.

Polhemus, Ted, *Streetstyle*, Thames and Hudson, 1995

Pollins, Harold, *Economic History of the Jews in England*, Fairleigh Dickenson University Press, 1982

Ross, Alan, *Ranji: Prince of cricketers*, Collins, 1983

Ross, Karen, *Black and White Media: Black images in popular film and television*, Polity Press, 1996

Shang, Anthony, *The Chinese in Britain*, Batsford, 1984

Tannahill, Reay, *Food in History*, Penguin Books, rev ed 1988

Tannahill, J A, *European Volunteer Workers in Britain*, Manchester University Press, 1958

Thomas, M and J Martin-Williams, *Overseas Nurses in Britain*

Vaz, Keith MP, *Still in the Shadows: A report into black and Asian appointments to public bodies*, House of Commons, May 1994

Visram, Rozina, *A History of the Asian Community in Britain*, Wayland Publishers, 1995

Visram, Rozina, *Ayahs, Lascars and Princes: Indians in Britain 1700-1947*, Pluto Press, 1986

Walvin, James, *Passage to Britain: Immigration in British history and politics*, Penguin Books, 1984

Weller, Paul, ed, *Religions in the UK: A multi-faith directory*, University of Derby in association with the Inter-Faith Network for the UK, 1993

Werbner, Pnina, 'Renewing an industrial past: British Pakistani entrepreneurship in Manchester,' in *Migration: The Asian Experience*, eds Judith M Brown and Rosemary Foot, St Martin's Press, 1994

INDEX OF NAMES

PICTURE SOURCES

Where more than one picture appears on a page, lowercase letters in alphabetical order indicate the sequence on the page, proceeding from left to right, top to bottom. The Commission for Racial Equality gratefully acknowledges the permission granted by copyright owners to reproduce the pictures used. Although every effort has been made to trace and contact copyright holders prior to publication, we have been unsuccessful in a few instances. If notified, the Commission for Racial Equality would be pleased to rectify any omissions at the earliest opportunity.

Andes Press Agency 35, 106a
Anthony Crickmay 121 (*Isabel Tamen and Kenneth Tharp in the London Contemporary Dance production,* Rikud)
Angela Taylor Photography 79a
Anthony Blake 58b, 62a, 62b
A F Kersting 9
Arcaid/David Churchill 108c
Arcaid/Richard Bryant 97c
Arcaid/Richard Waite 98a
BBC television services 31a, 86, 87b, 89, 90b, 90c, 103
Bradford History Research Unit 41a
Bill Cooper 71b
British Library 11
Brahm PR 48
Bridgeman Art Library 10,12, 15, 22, 54a, 83c* 85a, 98c, 99a, 99b, 100a
Brighton Reference Library 20 (2)
British Airways 52c
British Library 19
Caparo Group 44b
Chris Pillitz 57a
Christie's 60a, 100b
Chunchi Group 28b
College of Arms i*†,1,120†
Colorsport 37d, 64a, 64b*, 65c, 66a, 66b, 66c, 67b, 68a, 68b
Corbiss Bettmann 69b
CP Archives 114d
CRE 59b, 116e
Creative Hands/Frank Rogers 82b
Daily Express 114b
David Hoffman 1
David Richardson 106b
EMG Ltd. 43b
English Heritage 18
Essex County Cricket Club 65b
Faith Wilson 82a
Financial Times 47a
Finsbury Library 114a
Flamingo 94c
Format/Judy Harrison 108a
Format/Brenda Prince 56a, 56b
Format/Melanie Friend 53b

Fotomas 24
Fusion 58a
Guardian 113a
Guildhall Library 14
Herman Rodrigues 42a
Hilary Shedel 79b*
Hugo Glendinning 81a, 81b
Hull City Museums 17
Hulton Getty 23, 29b, 34, 61a, 67a, 85b, 104a, 104b, 104c, 111b, 115c
Images 107
Impact 61b
Impact/Piers Cavendish 42, 76b
Impact/Simon Shepheard 48c, 51, 69a
Imperial War Museum 27, 29a 30a, 30b, 30c*, 31b, 31c
Island Records 75a
Jerry Matthews 57b
John Birdsall 37a*, 55a
John Prince 49
Joseph King 87a
Kobal 90a
Laurie Lewis 78b
Lewis Photos Ltd 41b
Lewis Walpole Library/Yale University 19
Link Picture Library 39, 48a, 53a
Link/John Evans 53a
Lisson Gallery/Andrew Penketh 102a
London Features 74c, 77a
London Zoo 98b 59b, 78a
Lubiana Himid 102b
Mark Hendrick 116d
Mary Evans Picture Library 11, 22, 24, 63a, 65a, 70a, 83b, 83c, 115b
Michael Holford 5, 7
Mrs Cynthia Moody 101b
Museum of London, 7 14 16, 20, 21, 33a, 48b, 110c
National Maritime Museum 19
National Museum of Labour History, Manchester 25
Natural History Museum 21
Network/John Sturrock 45a
Network/Homer Sykes 3, 37c, 109, 111a
News Team/Dan Chung 97b

Niall McInerny 77b, 77c
NPG 20, 25, 26, 115a
PA Advertising 50
Performing Arts Library 72a, 72b, 72c, 93c
Performing Arts Library/Clive Barda 37e, 84c
Parachute Pictures/ David Browne 73a
Paul Herman 17
Penguin Books 94b, 105 b
Permindar Kaur 102c
Peter Walsh 45b
Phil May 60b
Pimlico Opera 71c
Photofusion/Janis Austin 3, 117
Picador 94a, 94c, 94d
Popperfoto 20, 96*
Pugwash/Sue England 54b
Redferns 74b 74d, 74e, 75b, 75c*
Red Features 101a
Ronald Grant Collection 71a, 73c, 74a, 87c, 93a
Routledge 105c
Royal Albert Memorial Museum, Exeter, 19
Sally Lancaster 55b
Somerville College, Oxford 112a
Sorabji Archive 70b
Steve Hanson 80a
Sun Alliance/MJ Adelmann 37b, 47b
Swiss Cottage Archives 113b
Terry Austin-Smith 105b
Theatro Technis 83a
Times 43
Tim Smith 52a, 108b
Topham 32, 40, 52b
Tottenham Hotspur 63b
Universal Pictorial 54c, 54d, 88a, 88b, 90c, 95a, 112b, 116a, 116b, 116c
Val Wilmer 73b, 101c
Virgin 76a
Wandsworth Library 114c
Welsh Industrial and Maritime Museum 28a
W K Luk 59a

---

* Image also used in the cover montage.
† Image reversed left-to-right.

COMMISSION FOR RACIAL EQUALITY

UNITING BRITAIN FOR A JUST SOCIETY

The Commission for Racial Equality was set up under the 1976 Race Relations Act. It receives an annual grant from the Home Office, but works independently of Government. The CRE is run by Commissioners appointed by the Home Secretary, and has support from all the main political parties.

The CRE has three main duties:

- To work towards the elimination of racial discrimination and to promote equality of opportunity

- To encourage good relations between people from different ethnic and racial backgrounds

- To monitor the way the Race Relations Act is working and recommend ways in which it can be improved

The CRE is the only Government-appointed body with statutory power to enforce the Race Relations Act.

The Commission for Racial Equality

is working for a just society

which gives everyone an equal

chance to learn, work and live

free from discrimination and

prejudice, and from the fear

of racial harassment and violence.

Head Office
Elliot House
10/12 Allington Street
London SW1E 5EH
☎ 0171-828 7022

Birmingham
Alpha Tower (11th Floor)
Suffolk Street Queensway
Birmingham B1 1TT
☎ 0121-632 4544

Leeds
Yorkshire Bank Chambers
(1st Floor)
Infirmary Street
Leeds LS1 2JP
☎ 0113-243 4413

Manchester
Maybrook House (5th floor)
40 Blackfriars Street
Manchester M3 2EG
☎ 0161-831 7782

Leicester
Haymarket House (4th Floor)
Haymarket Shopping Centre
Leicester LE1 3YG
☎ 0116-251 7852

Scotland
45 Hanover Street
Edinburgh EH2 2PJ
☎ 0131-226 5186

Wales
Pearl Assurance House
(14th floor)
Greyfriars Street
Cardiff CF1 3AG
☎ 01222-388977